I0101626

Diary
of an
Unkempt Woman

The irreverent thoughts of
Sandra Miller Linhart

LIONHEART GROUP PUBLISHING
PRINTED IN THE USA

Diary of an Unkempt Woman
irreverent thoughts of Sandra Miller Linhart

For information regarding permission, email Lionheart Group Publishing: permissions@lionheartgrouppublishing.com

Paperback ISBN: 978-1-938505-11-9

E-Book ISBN: 978-1-938505-22-5

Library of Congress Control Number: 2017908425

Text copyright © 1976-2017 by Sandra Miller Linhart, most previously published in her blog of the same title.
Cover art & Design copyright © 2017 by Sandi Linhart.
Edited by Betsy Beard
First Edition ~ August 2017

Published by Lionheart Group Publishing, Colorado, USA
Printed in the USA ~ All rights reserved.

visit us on the web at www.lionheartgrouppublishing.com

For the lonely.

Novels by This Author

Monica, Lost

Hallie of the Harvey Houses

Living with L.V. Brown

Visit the author's website at www.sandstarbooks.com

Preface (AKA Warning)

I started my blog, *The Diary of an Unkempt Woman*, in 2007 at the suggestion—make that the strongly encouraged suggestion—of my first-ever publisher, to get my name out there. Maybe? At any rate, I always did what I was told.

At first I penned trepidatiously, and then the weirdest yet nicest thing happened. The words began to flow from my head most ardently. However, the few who stumbled onto my blog, whether by chance or by stalking, frequently commented on my misgivings and horribly marred personality. Apparently, I was *the* most cynical individual to have ever penned a thought or perception. I've created a gold-embossed plaque to adorn my office wall and commemorate this achievement, a significant accomplishment if you ask me—the award, not the creation of one. Maybe both.

Much of what I wrote fell into the category of irony, humor, and the astutely absurd. The darker side of the human soul shadowed some of my stories and thoughts. But I've never written anything to be purely spiteful, malicious, or unkind... as far as you know. I've not claimed to be anyone I'm not. At that time in my life, I called 'em as I seed 'em. Unfortunately for my readers, I was a bit myopic and mostly blind.

I think I'm funny. But as my mom is wont to say, "Looks aren't everything."

Well, times change, and we change, thankfully. I've since removed the majority of these posts from my blog and turned over a new leaf. But, I compiled a few of my eclectic favorites into this book just because I feel it's a sin to destroy creative art, regardless of content. I've included short stories, essays (formerly blog posts), and poems (some of which I wrote in the late 1970s, chock-full of a high schooler's angsty thoughts, hopes, and dreams) most penned between 2007 and 2016, an especially bleak decade of my life, apparently.

I fall way short of being the best writer. I hope you'll find I'm not the worst, though. Who knows? Maybe one of the mental sketches between these covers will pull you in and cause you to ponder for more than just a minute.

Please visit my website: www.sandstarbooks.com.

Enjoy & In Joy

Diary
of an
Unkempt Woman

Heinz 57

The English language is such a diverse and wonderful thing. It can distract you, confuse you, and bring you to tears of laughter when arranged in one way or another. That's why I think I love it so... and hate it so.

For instance, take the word *wind*. It stands for storm, blustery weather, breeze, and also coil, twist, curl, and wrap around. But wait, I'm not done yet. It can mean snake, meander, bend, and curve (among others). So... if I were to say, "Wind the wind," would you take it to mean I want you to twist the breeze, or storm the snake? As you know, snake can also mean reptile or curve. How confusing is that? And only I, as the creator of the sentence know for sure, right? You can give an educated guess to what I mean by it, but until I tell you what I mean (flat out or in other ways) you'll never truly know. You can only speculate.

I love when I can write a book and each person who reads it injects little of his or her life into it. *Daddy's Boots* and *Momma's Boots* are fine examples. The main character in each picture book is gender non-specific, yet everyone who's read them, without exception, pictured the main character as a boy if their child is a boy, or as a girl if their child is a girl. That's the magic, the wonderment of the written word; the written story.

It's also a detriment to a story—from any storyteller, seasoned or raw. I mean something completely innocent in writing "He aggressively spackled his way to the end of the crowded hall." But if you don't know what *spackled* means, you could come up with maybe three or four actions he may be taking as he would wind (meander) down the crowded, windy (curved) hall. (You more than likely *do* know what *spackled* means now that DYI programs are such a hit, but I digress.)

I could write a story about a little six-year-old boy named Russy, who took a balloon to the top of an old, gutted-out barn to release it into the breeze hoping someone in Denmark might find it, and connect with him in some magical way. And you could inevitably remember yourself in a similar situation as a child (as close as you can get, anyway) and attach the appropriate-to-you feelings of danger, hope, expectation, and wonder.

But what if someone you loved fell off a barn roof and died? Would my innocent words then cause fear and anxiety, loss, anguish, and discomfort? I believe they would. And the closer you were to the accident or the deceased, the stronger those feelings are sure to be.

What if you grew up in a big city where barns are scarce? Would you picture a big, red monstrosity or a small, rectangular horse shack? It makes a difference to the story, doesn't it? I mean, if Russy climbed ten feet in the air to release a balloon, well that's not nearly as scary as climbing up the ladder, shimmying onto the broadside, and making his way up the slight, but ever-so-dangerous, pitch of the barn roof fifty feet from death—all with a balloon grasped tightly in his sweaty, cramping hand.

[He's been holding on to the string so tightly. He doesn't want to release it until he can attach the paper holding his identity. Which is in his... Did he remember to grab it off the table as he rushed out the door? Did he put it in his pocket?]

What feelings emanated from thinking he might have gotten nearly all the way to the top of the barn roof, only to discover he'd forgotten his name? [See what I did there?

He didn't truly forget his name—only the piece of paper on which his name is written.]

Don't you hate that feeling? Getting somewhere crucial, like a business meeting, just in the nick of time, not a moment to spare, and Oops! Forgot the main presentation!

Did the words put feelings into your mind and memory, or did your associations to those words do the trick?

If you walked into a bakery, would the counter girl with a pimply face and braces who handed you your biscuit remind you of your grandma's cooking? Or would the hot, melty aroma bring your memories smack dab back into the warmth of her kitchen and heart?

But what if your grandma was a meanie-boobaleenie who ate the biscuits in front of you and wouldn't share, even though the cupboards were bare? Yeah, you wouldn't be so happy in the bakery then, would you?

The same words can mean plethora things to different humans, whether spoken or written. We use our own assumptions and beliefs to interpret the words we read and hear. It happens all the time in books, in magazine articles, and in presidential speeches.

Most of the time we never truly know what an author meant, or what he or she *meant* their words to imply. Because once them-that-know grab a hold of it, it goes hog-wild crazy. Mouths start screaming, words start spewing, and...

Everyone.

Stops.

Hearing.

For every written word at least five meanings can be attached. For every sentence, probably fifty-seven interpretations. For every feeling the author tries to capture and convey, you attach your history, your feelings, your upbringing, your desires, your dreams, your disappointments, your humiliations, your fears, your anger...and sometimes your feelings about the author as a person.

If you picked up a book by Stephen King, you'd assume you're going to get the shit scared out of you, and would more than likely be disappointed when you discovered he'd written a romance novel. But still, at every turn of the page you'd anticipate a monster lurking in the shadows.

If you believed the author wrote with hate and destruction, you'd feel that hate embedded in his words. The doors and windows of your soul would slam shut.

But if you began reading without any preconceived notions about the author or story, the windows fling wide and the doors sweep open, allowing you the full pleasure of the taste of each and every word.

In many ways, a writer is a chef who creates a masterpiece for you to devour; always hoping you'll take something away you enjoyed and savor until the next course.

Bon Appétit.

I'm Told I Don't Come Across Well

There's a reason I seldom leave home.

There's a reason I stay far away from people.

There's a reason I don't get close and keep my distance.

There's a reason...

So don't come into *my* world and tell me
I'm rubbing *you* the wrong way.

My world doesn't touch yours,

And I never invited you in.

So stop reading my blog.

You click on the bookmark

no referring link

so you can find something which incites you

between my words?

You love to hate me.

Me... the mother of your offspring?

The one who got away?

The reason for your failed relationships?

The reason for your failed life?

The reason you burnt your toast this morning?

Me?

So stop reading my blog.

You think my words are directed at you.

You anon yourself into my blog.

You cajole and you quip;

You twist and you turn and you lie

safely

warmly

snuggly

inside the blanket of a mask

you stab me with your keyboard.

You know who I am.

I'm the reason you're miserable.

I'm the reason you fight.

I'm the reason you can't sleep at night.

Me...without even trying.

I

am

just

sitting

here

putting

one

word

after

another

on

this

page...

You read the words and go berserk:

"What a moron! What a jerk!"

"What a worthless piece of work!"

So... stop reading my blog.

I write to express, to talk, to feel

...something.

A gift I've not had access to in my non-virtual world

as I feel my soul slowly dying,

like my skin—shriveling up and thinning, blotchy, tired

...and so very much alone, untouched.

Words I speak aloud are seldom heard;

they fall to the floor and seep into the cracks

where they cushion the soles

of the people I pick up after.

...until I put them down here

and you read them

and decide for yourself what I'm saying

and it's never pretty.

for you *don't* see me as pretty

you *can't* see me as pretty

you *won't* see me as pretty

...on the inside.

So... stop reading my blog.

I write for myself

I write of my feelings, my thoughts and my fears.

I don't write for you.

I don't even know who *you* are.

Were we once friends?

Did you once care?

Because if so, I don't know you anymore...

and you most certainly don't know me,

...if you ever did.

Stop reading my blog.

Eng1A

The rain beats down upon the cold, hard ground and splatters into fine mist on impact, mixing with the spray from other spherical pellets falling from the dark sky. Each droplet leaves a minute, singular pit in the hard, packed earth, making its mark until another falls to succeed it. Soon the ground is covered with a fine layer of muddy-colored water, and a faint cloud of mist.

As the skies grow darker. The temperature falls. The rain endures in a silent repetitive vibration without an audience. The thin film covering the ground steadily rises as the downpour continues. Little rivers of water rush toward the growing cracks in the softened earth, leaving their own marks among the sand and rocks on their way to joining others. The pools nervously huddle in low spots as if to stay warm in the bite of the evening. The frigid night air surrounds them. A thin crust of ice gradually creeps around their edges, leaving a slight shimmer like a dancing ballerina in the moonlight.

Subtly, in the bitter torrent of rain, a quietness overcomes the night. The downpour subsides to a fine drizzle, then to nothingness. A monotonous drip beats a staccato tune in the dark distance, filling the silence with its stubbornness. The glacial huddle of gathering water relaxes in the stillness, patiently awaiting the rising sun and the warmth it provides.

(1982)

Monster's Ball

When did children become such a focal point in our personal worlds? Such a dichotomy we are... Johnny down the street gets beaten every day behind closed doors and we look the other way. Little Cindy gets raped by her step-dad and we act like she deserved it (I wonder what she did to set him off, or did you see what she was wearing?). Schools dictate the Department of Education's idea of good nutrition to our children and we blindly believe them.

We expect the school system to raise our children, but under our individual rules. And, apparently, your child is the center of the Universe, bar none. The rest of us are supposed to bow down and kiss his feet.

I know a boy, about four, who's allowed free range of our neighborhood. His next-door neighbor is building an addition onto his house, so building materials linger here and there. I don't think that's against the law.

Monster (a name I've lovingly endowed upon the boy) runs up to the windows stacked against the wall and kicks the glass out. Isn't he cute?

He then takes a trip to the little pond on the grassy knoll, kicks dirt in on the fish. He tries to catch them by their tails. When that activity bores him, he knocks the rocks off the waterfall element. How adorable!

When his parents call on their neighbor, Monster runs amok, uncensored. He breaks wine glasses, pulls wires out of the wall, and jumps on the antique furniture. What a doll!

The thing is, Monster's parents pay no attention to his bad behavior.

I've watched Monster kick his mother's head and slug her in the stomach. She 'disciplines' him by screaming at him to stop, then ignores him when he doesn't...which is her prerogative. I don't think that's against the law.

But when Monster's family visited neighbor last, Mr. Neighbor asked Monster's parents to reel in and stop Monster's bad behavior, or Mr. N would.

Mr. N replaced his sidewalk lights twice because of Monster. He estimated the lovely child cost him over a thousand dollars in damages this year alone.

When Monster ran up and started jumping on the cistern, Mr. N asked again they control their child. Mr. N feared Monster might cut himself on the glass he breaks, fall into the little pond, hit his head and drown, or fall off the top of the addition Mr. N is building.

If any of these scenarios came to fruition, who do you think would be sued?

What did my sister call that? Desirable Nuisance? Attractive Nuisance. Something like that. If you have a covered pool in your yard, within a locked fence and signage around, and a kid scales your fence, wanders in and drowns, you can be sued for owning an Attractive Nuisance. That *is* the law.

Well, Mr. N picked up Monster and swatted him on the butt. Not hard at all. Mother Monster became indignant and stomped off, son in tow. She hasn't been back to visit Mr. N since, but evidence of Monster's presence keeps showing up at Mr. N's: the fish need a bath, the waterfall again needs rebuilding, more construction supplies destroyed. And broken sidewalk lights...again.

When I was a child, we respected our elders as they earned it.

Now that I'm an adult, it puzzles me society gives respect to our children, unearned.

I respect my children, but not to the point of losing my self-respect. My children don't run my household. I don't discuss what we're going to do and get their permission to do it. I have over forty-five years of experience in life. My child has much less.

Why should I place adult burdens on my children by asking them if they think it's a good thing to, say, sell my house? Or what time they'd like to go to bed. Or whether or not they can have a friend spend the night.

And when they get an answer, it's done. Yes means yes. No means no. Not negotiable. *And if you pout or plead, guess where you're going to be spending the next fifteen or more minutes.*

Asking their opinions or desires is one thing. Contorting your life around their wants is a whole 'nuther animal.

I had to stop in at the drugstore last night with my two youngest. Youngest one has yet another ear infection. We submitted our prescriptions and walked the aisles—I guess so I could get the phrase, "No, we don't need it," out of my system. And maybe the girls needed to get the words, "Please, can we get this?" out of theirs.

Anyhoo, a mother was there with three young children ranging in age from about three to nine. The kids roamed all over the store, tossing balls from the racks and fighting over the vibrating pad on the chair.

"Mommy? Is it my turn yet? Tell Sissy it's my turn."

Mommy patiently, responsibly, and dutifully ignored them.

I stood in line at the pharmacy, awaiting my turn to pick up the prescriptions. I had a cart full of... okay, you caught me. Maybe I didn't say "no" to every request. Besides, we *needed* more candy to pass out for Halloween. And we *needed* the crystal ball-thingy with the witch's head that cackled and writhed when you pushed the button. And we *did* need the shampoo.

Anyhoo, I placed my foot in front of the wheel of the cart so it wouldn't roll back and forth to my daughter's impatient leaning against the cart.

"Why are we here again?"

"Because you need medicine. So shut up already."

No, I don't actually talk to them like that, but I want to sometimes.

"We have to get your medicine," is what I said.

Meanwhile, middle monster tossed a ball into the air and ran to catch it, both eyes on the ball (which is silly...unless he's one of those fish who has an eye on each side of its flat head) and crashed into the front of our cart.

Then the little sh...er...wonderful child ran up to his mother crying, pointing at me and said I ran my cart into him.

Attentive Mother glared at me. At me!

So I stuck my tongue out and said, "And I'd do it again!"

And when the boy went to sit down, I tripped him.

No, not really.

She glared at me.

I looked the other way.

...because I am a weanie.

Make-A-Hope

My sister told me she wants to win the lottery so she can give lots of money to the Make-A-Wish Foundation and I lost it (not temper, tears).

Why do the little cherubs who've been encased in love the entire 1825 days (plus or minus) on Earth get to have their wishes come true, only to depart this world and go to what all religions see as the ultimate wish: Heaven?

Whereas the tender little American souls whose fathers and mothers work 24/7 to make ends meet, don't usurp social programs, but cannot afford to buy new clothing, much less a trip to Disneyland...or the tender little ones who are beaten behind closed doors daily because Daddy or Mommy is a bully or on drugs (alcohol is a drug). What of these little beings who try so hard to please, who so much want to be loved or noticed? They get to live in quiet desperation, hoping someday their lives will get better. They dare to wish on one falling star after another, only to find out ten years later their wishes were wasted on a meteor. Not even a star. And when they've struggled through life, through disappointment after disappointment (no matter how high they've held their chin or how much they continued to hope and strive for a better life), they die at ninety, never having seen the ocean or a new pair of shoes or a wish come true.

What's the answer, though?

Suppose we made a Make-A-Hope Foundation for these tiny people? Would they be happier after seeing the world one day, if they had to come back to their existence of day-by-day? Or would they see the world for what it has to offer and then strive harder to make a better life for themselves as they grow up? Would kindness make their hearts grow bitter, knowing what they've been missing?

I have no answers.

I wish I could take all those awkward little (somewhat) healthy souls with scabbed knees and hand-me-down lives and give them a reason to hope, to believe, and to never give up. No matter how many times they're hit or discouraged or belittled or abused.

I wish I could wrap my arms around them and tell them, "This isn't what life is supposed to be. You drew the short straw, so pick your teeth with it and dare to be happy. This, too, shall pass."

So sue me already. Call me a pathetic, lifeless, ignorant idiot because I don't see any value in the Make-A-Wish Foundation. That's okay, because there are many people who do—and that's all MAWF needs, caring, loving people to donate to their cause.

When I make my millions, I'm going to donate to American children who fall through the cracks, and nobody notices anymore—much like the utility poles which line a busy street.

My Daughter, Jack

Daughter #4, Jo, was invited to a friend's birthday party at the local fitness club. She made a birthday card and donned her suit, all in front of Daughter #5, Sophē, who struggled to understand why she couldn't go, too. She was, after all, eight; only two years younger than Jo.

"It's not a community pool," I said.

"Yeah," Jo interjected. "Matt's family owns it. It has a huge hot tub, too."

"No, they do not. Jo quit teasing your sister."

I got a big smile as Jo ran to grab her towel.

"They won't notice." I sensed Sophē actually believed her words.

"Right…"

We dropped Jo at the fitness center and headed off on a quest for those non-skid thingies, probably made in China, you adhere to the floor of your bathtub so your kids (or Mom) won't slip and kill themselves in the shower. Do you know what they're called?

Nope, me neither.

So I walked through the first department store (no, not Wal-Mart) and finally asked someone who needed to ask someone, who told me, "Yeah, they're in the back with the shower curtains and stuff."

Duh.

I found a pretty shower curtain… needed one anyway. Looked all over for those thingies, and wished, not for the first time, I knew their exact moniker.

(Found an old, ugly, thick bath mat with octopus suction cups… offered in a beautiful shade of retirement-home-gray. I had to pass it up.)

We left Store # 1 with shower curtain, drain stopper (my bathtub drain leaks), and a child's make-up kit Sophē just *had to have*. It was on sale — 30% off — so that made it understandable, right? And besides, she didn't get to go swimming, and she promised she'd share with Jo as long as Jo was nice, and said please and didn't try to… (I admit. I stopped listening.)

Store # 2: Grocery store. No luck there.

Store # 3: Drugstore. No rude lady with three unruly kids, but no non-skiddy sticky stuff there either.

As Sophē and I exited the store, we passed a bin with a sign "ON SALE — 3/$10." The bin held plastic, personalized cups with the most up-to-date, popular names you could ever imagine… except my kids' names. Well, they had Paige but no Danna, Peanut, Jo or Sophē. Go figure. Sophē looked up at me and said "We gotta get this one for Paige."

Now remember, she didn't get to go swimming with her sister. And swimming was her favorite, number one sport of all time…

Rooting through the bargain bin, I thought, *Maybe I can find one for one of the cousins, or something we can use as a present later. Three for ten dollars…Wow! That's, like, too good to pass up… a little, crappy plastic cup for about $3.33. I'll give Paige the one for $3.34. Forget we don't need them. They're cheap at twice the price.*

Sophē pulled out a cup which said, "Sophia"

"I want this one," she declared.

"That's not your name," I said.

"So what? It's close enough."

"Close enough doesn't count in names."

"What do you mean?" She asked, still holding the cup.

"Sophia is not your name. I don't know any Sophias."

She looked at me with sad eyes which said, "Yeah, but I didn't get to go swimming..."

"We might as well get one that says 'Jack,'" I said.

"Who's Jack?" She asked.

Exactly my point.

Yeah, we left the store with three cups—one of which said Sophia—but I decided I'm going to start calling her Jack anyway.

What's in a name? (Unless you're trying to find something specific... like those stick-on non-skid bathtub thingies... which, apparently, my town doesn't have.)

Barriers

I close my eyes

And see you

Standing so near,

But when I look

Something's changed.

Maybe if I were blind

I wouldn't notice

The space

I keep putting

Between us,

And everything would be fine,

Like before.

For what is one

Man's handicap

Might be another's

Happiness.

~ age 16 (1979)

Sandy Really

(A Modern-Day Cinderella Story)

Not yesterday…

But a while ago…

There was a plain, ordinary little girl. Her blond hair played wildly upon her head, making it impossible to tame. Freckles sprayed her cheeks and nose like paint.

An unremarkable girl in all respects.

And her name was Sandy Really.

Sandy Really lived on the outskirts of a small rundown town in an adequate but small rundown house in the middle of a small rundown field. In fact, everything about the Wyoming town was rundown…the pool, the school, the store. Everything.

Sandy Really's mother did her best to make their rundown house a comfortable home. She sewed curtains from bright purple, green, and pink material. She taught Sandy Really how to sew, and together they mended and brightened up the place.

Mrs. Really also cooked the most wonderful treats and meals. She soon taught Sandy to cook, too, telling her someday, somewhere, Sandy Really would make a good Partner In Life.

Sandy Really learned to scrub and clean the rundown house into a shiny rundown home.

She planted beautiful flowers and bushes to cover the cracks in the sidewalks and walls outside their home.

She painted stems over the cracks on the walls inside and painted beautiful flowers to match the brilliant curtains.

Sandy Really knew what made things beautiful, and spent her days growing up practicing her art.

There was nothing Sandy Really couldn't do. Like her mom, she could build and paint. She could mend and sew. She knitted. She washed. She planted and gardened and cooked what she grew into tasty treats. The Really's home glowed with love.

One day not long ago...

But not yesterday...

Mrs. Really told her daughter to leave their home to find a Partner in Life. She said the best place to find a partner to love and respect you for who you are was in college.

So at the age of seventeen, like most girls, Sandy Really scolded her hair with a brush, covered her freckles with brown face paste, and headed off to college.

She drank in the knowledge of books and listened carefully to men and women in long robes who spoke of things she'd never even imagined.

She didn't look hard for a Partner in Life, but every time she talked to her mother, she heard how important it was to find the perfect one.

Right before she left the college with a diploma, Sandy Really realized she had failed her mother. She had knowledge, but not a Partner in Life.

She knew she didn't have much time. School would soon be finished, and everyone would be going home. She'd go back to her small rundown house in the middle of a small rundown field on the outskirts of the small rundown town in Wyoming... where finding a Partner in Life would be next to impossible.

Sandy Really took her head from her books and looked around.

People surrounded her.

They were learning.

They laughed and talked.

They shared ideas—like the men and women in long robes who taught her. She joined in and soon found herself in a group of people called Friends.

Sandy Really never had Friends before and was thrilled with the feeling. She spoke and they listened. They spoke and she listened. Sometimes they disagreed. Sometimes they agreed. But always they smiled and shared and welcomed other's thoughts and feelings. Sandy Really started learning more about life from these talks than she did from her mother or the men and women in long robes.

Tom Twiddle was one of these Friends. Tom Twiddle made a special effort to stand next to Sandy Really. Tom listened and agreed with everything Sandy said. Soon Sandy found herself alone with Tom and felt something she had never felt before. Tom was rich and smart, everything Mrs. Really had said Sandy Really wanted in a Partner in Life.

And before she knew it, Sandy Really became Mrs. Twiddle.

Mrs. Twiddle found herself in a beautiful house with no need for paint.

There were no cracks in the walls, inside or out. None in the sidewalks. No place to plant food or flowers.

There were other people in the house who took care of things like that.

Tom Twiddle forbade Mrs. Twiddle to paint, but he allowed her to cook. Mrs. Twiddle cooked the most incredible meals for Tom Twiddle. And he allowed her to sew, so she sewed the most elaborate robes for him. He allowed her to clean, so she kept his house spotless and did everything her mother taught her to keep her partner happy.

And Tom Twiddle was happy.

But Mrs. Twiddle was not.

Nobody spoke to her anymore. No one listened to what

she said. Mrs. Twiddle felt lonely in her beautiful house full of people.

Mrs. Twiddle's fingers throbbed at the end of the day from mending Tom Twiddle's favorite clothes. Her back ached from polishing his floor into the shine he prided. Her hands wore blisters from making his favorite meals in the oven.

Mrs. Twiddle sat on the couch next to Tom Twiddle and snuggled up to his side. Tom Twiddle pushed her away and said the game was about over, but could she be a dear and get him a snack?

Yes, Mrs. Twiddle was a good Partner in Life, but Tom Twiddle was not.

The day came when she found herself back in the small rundown house in the middle of the small rundown field on the outskirts of the small rundown town in Wyoming.

She gave back Tom Twiddle's name and became Sandy Really once again.

Sandy Really liked being home at first. Then she grew sad and lonely. She missed the big, beautiful home she shared with Tom Twiddle. She yearned to talk to friends again.

Mrs. Really saw her daughter's pain and told her to go to the city to find a job...and maybe a new and different Partner in Life.

A while ago...

But not yesterday...

Sandy Really set off for the big city. At first she was afraid because she left the small rundown town on a small rundown bus, but as the bus got closer and closer to the big city, Sandy Really thought the city looked a lot like her old rundown town, only bigger...

Much bigger.

The bus station in the city was as rundown as the one in her rundown town, only bigger...

Much bigger.

Sandy Really found a small rundown apartment in the big

city, next to a small rundown restaurant where she found a job. She went from table to table and got people what they asked for.

If they were nice people, they left her spare change.

If they weren't, they left her nothing.

Luckily for Sandy Really, most of the people who ate at the restaurant were nice and soon Sandy Really had a decent apartment, filled with little trinkets to make her happy.

In the small rundown restaurant next to her decent apartment worked a cook named Gary Greatest. Sandy Really liked Gary Greatest. He made her laugh until she couldn't stand up. Gary Greatest lived in a decent apartment near hers, and soon they became good friends. They went to the movies together and talked all night long about what Gary Greatest thought was right with the world. And like the last time, before she knew what happened Sandy Really turned into Mrs. Greatest.

Now, strange things happen to some people when they find themselves with any old Partner in Life. Mrs. Greatest knew Tom Twiddle had changed, but she never thought Gary Greatest would.

And yet he did.

He liked to drink brown liquid from a bottle, and when he did it a lot, Gary Greatest became bad. Gary Greatest broke Mrs. Greatest's little trinkets. He shouted names at her and sold most of her things for more of the bottled brown liquid. At night, Mrs. Greatest was not only sore from working, cooking, and cleaning, but also from bruises and marks Gary Greatest left on her when he had too much of the brown liquid.

Mrs. Greatest was lonely. She didn't have anyone to talk to.

And she was scared.

Once again, Sandy gave Gary Greatest back his name and became Sandy Really.

But Sandy Really didn't return to the small rundown house in the middle of the small rundown field on the outskirts of the small rundown town in Wyoming. Instead, she found a nice apartment in a pretty part of the city and started working in a tall building down the block. She was smart, after all, and could use what she learned from college at her new job. She liked the people there and enjoyed talking with them.

She soon forgot all about Tom Twiddle and Gary Greatest.

Sandy Really worked hard at the job she loved and soon had a beautiful house of her own. It had no cracks, but she still painted flowers on the walls. She could afford curtains, but she sewed her own out of purple, green, and pink material anyway. She didn't need them, but she planted a garden of vegetables and grew flowers, too.

She let her hair play wildly on her head and stopped covering her freckles with brown face paste.

Sandy Really was happy for the first time since leaving her small rundown home in the middle of the small rundown field on the outskirts of the small rundown town in Wyoming.

Not yesterday…

But before…

Sandy Really wasn't looking for a Partner in Life anymore, but she met someone anyway. Robbie Reliable worked next to Sandy Really in the big office building. They became good friends and soon Robbie Reliable moved into Sandy Really's beautiful home.

This time, Sandy Really stayed Sandy Really.

And Robbie remained Reliable.

Robbie and Sandy both cooked when they wanted to eat. And they both cleaned when they needed to clean. They painted and planted and shared ideas. And they laughed together. And they smiled together. And sometimes they cried together, but not for long. Robbie and Sandy's home glowed with love.

Sandy then knew what her mother meant when she told her to go out and find a Partner in Life. And Sandy knew Robbie was the right partner for her.

But to this day...
Yes, even yesterday...
Remarkably, she is still just Sandy.
Really.

Blissless

Frightened faces,

Peering,

Hoping not to see

What is showing,

But

Wanting to know

The truth

Just the same.

~ age 14 (1976)

You Have How Many Kids?

I recently returned from a conference where I met quite a few people.

You've been to these things, right? You go to the sessions and write down notes you know you'll probably never look at again unless and until, years later, you're looking for something totally unrelated and come across them. And you read them over and think, *Oh, yeah. I remember this speaker* or *that topic.* Then you put it back in the pile to be found the next time you're looking for something else totally unrelated, but until then promptly forgotten.

After the different workshops, we typically milled around and shared small-talk.

Eventually someone would ask me about my family. I'd tell them I have five kids and they'd raise their eyebrow.

I know what they're thinking. Either they're my age and remember the zero-population-growth goal or—

Wait! Please allow me to go off on a tangent. I'll get back to my kids. I promise.

Al Gore recently won the Nobel Peace Prize for... um, I'm not sure. But I know I'll never feel the same about this prize ever again. Unless, of course, I win. And then it will rise again in my esteem to the quality and awe it once held. Anyway, he thought up this wonderful way for the ultra-rich to feel good about their wasteful energy consumption, apparently by paying some large corporation the amount of money equal to the carbon footprint on which each wasteful person impacts this earth.

In turn, this corporation is supposed to use this money to work on lowering pollution in one way or another. I know I've boiled this down to a nutshell, but that's basically the idea of the footprint fallacy.

I have a few problems with this. You know, things that don't compute?

First: Just because you pay a few bucks (comparative to your income), your energy waste doesn't decrease. It only makes you feel better about being wasteful. The more energy you waste = the more money you contribute = the better Americans you are. Pat yourselves on the backs.

Second: Huh?

Third: Soon all the energy waste and carbon footprint culpability will be placed on Joe Schmoe who is only trying to make ends meet, can't afford gasoline so he walks to work, grows his own vegetable garden because he doesn't have the money for food, and is too proud to take food stamps or welfare. He won't be able to even pay the... oh, I don't know, let's just say one hundred dollars a month to zero out his carbon footprint. Therefore, all of these wonderful SUV driving, million-dollar-home owning, fly-across-the-world-for-a-burger people will be secure in the knowledge they did their part to make this world a better, greener place.

Damn you, Joe Schmoe. You're ruining our country. Off with your head!

Now, I hate to pop misconceptions, but Al Gore did not come up with this concept.

Back in 1987, when I had my third child (which screwed up the zero-population growth initiative touted by the media at the time) I came up with a brilliant plan:

Daughter #1, Danna aligns under me.

Daughter #2, Peanut aligns under her father.

My brother, a wonderful and brilliant man, decided years

ago he never wanted to father a child, thereby allowing me to place daughter #3, Peaches in line with his column.

Voila!

Zero population growth—no offspring footprint. I am in alignment with the "good" people of the United States.

(I've since screwed up this incredible strategy by birthing two more females. Does anybody have an empty column or two to sell, so I can feel better about myself?)

I think I'll sue Gore for stealing my idea.

Unless, of course, he thought of it before 1987, which suggests he takes an awful long time to implement a plan.

Have you noticed the media has since all but abandoned the zero-population growth scheme? I wonder why. It does take the onus from me, however. Life is good.

Okay. I'm done. Back to the main point of the story (if I ever had one.)

—either they're my age and remember the zero-population-growth goal, or they're ten or so years younger than me, and raised in a time when it became the in-thing to wait until your thirties to have a child.

I'd always get the same responses:

"Five children?"

"Yes. And all girls."

"All girls? Bless your heart."

Okay, another tangent...

I lived in the South from 1999 to 2005. I've heard "bless your heart" too many times to mention. After observing and watching, I learned the true meaning of the phrase. It means: You're so stupid.

Stay with me here.

You see someone trip.

A proper woman walks over and helps them up saying:

"You tripped on that little ol' thing? Why, bless your heart."

Someone spills coffee down their front. You hear the person next to them say: "Oh, my goodness. That coffee is hot. Did you get burnt? Bless your heart."

And then, as I said: "You have five girls? Bless your heart."

Don't take my word for it. Try it out. The next time you hear "bless your heart" fill in the words "you're so stupid" and see if they fit. In my experience, they fit like a glove. And now, back to my story.

They'd raise their other eyebrow. Then the conversation would go either one way or another: "What are their ages" or, my personal favorite, "You gonna try for a boy?"

Again, I say, "Huh?"

Am I going to try for a boy?

At such question, I'd facepalm and say, "Damn! Why didn't I try for a boy when I had the chance?"

Then: "You don't look like a mother of five." (Thank you, but I've always wondered and never asked, how *is* a mother of five supposed to look?) Or: "Wow, you must have started early in life."

I was twenty-two when I had Danna. I grew up in a little Wyoming town. All of my friends and associates were married with kids by the time they were nineteen. I was considered 'an old maid' when I married at twenty-one. Nowadays this is considered (in most American cultures) to be too young and girls are encouraged to wait until at least their late twenties to be married and into their thirties to become mothers.

I did both. Kids in my early twenties and kids in my mid-late thirties. I've been a mother of prepubescent female children for over three decades.

Bless my heart.

A Friend

Friends

Fall when

You trip.

Friends

Keep spiders

Off your back.

It's a tough job

Being a friend.

I should know.

I

Am

One.

~ age 15 (1978)

Rainy Days and Mondays

I pondered giving the little ones their umbrellas as it looked like rain outside this morning. It reminded me of an incident years ago involving my three older daughters when they were much younger.

I had recently married my second husband and his father took my three daughters (from my previous marriage) shopping. Danna would have been—hold on while I do the math—about eight, placing Peanut in the age seven category, and Peaches at five.

The brandy-new grandpa came back from shopping overly impressed by Peaches' choice. He explained he had taken them to a store, told them all to go find something they wanted and he would purchase it for them. They had no way of knowing it was a test of their character—the first of many.

I cannot recall what the older two wanted, as they obviously chose incorrectly, but Peaches was hailed as "*the* unselfish one" when she picked a child's umbrella. Grandpa apparently tried to talk her into something less practical, more hedonistic, but Peaches stuck to her desire to have the small, red and white striped *Hello Kitty* umbrella. Grandpa left the store, seemingly impressed and continued to talk of the incident until his death about three years later (unrelated).

My children learned a hard lesson that day—a lesson I don't deem as a true or fair one, but a lesson in humility all the same. Every episode in their lives from that day forward would be judged and labeled by that family for the rest of their lives.

Choosing something functional wasn't Peaches' goal. Impressing her new grandpa wasn't even in the cards, but she drew the correct one and was labeled for life as the (only) unselfish child of mine for all time, fit to be a true member of their family. (I never passed that test, by the way.)

I learned a lesson that day as well. I learned the two types of love: a parent's love, which is unconditional, and the fake "I love you as long as you act and do as I approve" love, which is what we all lived with over the past two decades.

Of all the experiences I've had in my life and shared with my kids, I wish I might have foreseen the effects of that family's conditional love on my children's lives. I wish I would've nipped it in the bud and instead taught them the true meaning of love.

Until I met this family I never knew every episode in life, every choice you make, and every word you speak would be a test of your character. I never knew choosing something off the shelf might speak directly to your worth.

Frailty, mistakes, learning, bad choices, redemption, forgiveness, humanity...all words inaccessible and actions unforgivable by that family.

I didn't know most people were born perfect.

Someday, I'll take my grandson to the store and let him pick something off the shelves. The more hedonistic and useless, the better...and I'll never make him feel bad about his choice.

I didn't give the little ones their umbrellas this morning. In fact, they rarely use them except to play. A little rain never hurt anyone.

The truth is I can't look at an umbrella without feeling a pang of shame and regret.

Searching

Stars like diamonds, dressed in black,

Shine upon the world's great back.

Dropping light for all to see,

Luring me, yes, luring me.

Making me believe in space,

And another social race.

Though it may sound strange to hear,

I dream of often being there.

Out there in the vast beyond,

For me there is no greater bond,

So strong, so deep —a grasping lure,

Like nothing else, to be sure.

I'll follow dreams and ne'er fail

To make sound this thought-up tale,

That out there in the great unknown

Is all that is, but never shown.

Who? A mortal being as I

To think that I might really fly

Above the rest who will not try?

My life's a riddle, now you know

But to the stars I dare must go.

I'll fight my mortal binds aside

And from inside I'll find my guide.

Who knows? Maybe you and me

Are the chosen ones to flee.

~ age 14 (1976)

Carl's Bad Caverns and
Other Dead Mammals

A few years ago, I took my mother, my aunt, and my two youngest daughters to New Mexico on a road trip. Our first stop was Roswell, New Mexico, where we visited an exhibition of my mother's favorite topic ever—aliens and UFOs—and were privileged to sit in on an alien autopsy.

Dead aliens. How freaky is that? We spent hours and hours looking over their exhibits, my mom in her own special alien heaven. We spent so much time, in fact, I was beginning to become apathetic toward them. How many wrecked silver disks, little green men, and alternative theories can you take in one day, anyway? We spent the night in Roswell, with a plan to drive to Carlsbad the next day.

It turned out the freakiest thing about Roswell had nothing to do with little green men, however. That particular moniker was saved for a medium-sized blue man in the early morning hours.

As we were driving out of town, I noticed a taped-off partition in front of a local bank, with yellow DO NOT CROSS police ribbon. At the center of this cordoned area was a mannequin-esque male figure on his back with his arms and feet in the air, knees bent; the position one would take when crawling, but strangely inverted.

(We discovered later the indigent vagabond had frozen to death during the night.)

I remember his left foot was without shoe. The sock he

wore on it shone a bright white in the rising sun.

Talk about a surreal experience. When you think about people finding bodies, or people seeing death, you don't think of a body in the front yard of a local bank, frozen stiff with rigor mortis, legs and arms in the air; police officers milling around talking, ignoring the corpse in their presence.

Thank God the girls didn't see him.

Dead aliens in a museum have nothing in the freaky-factor compared to a dead man in a bank yard.

The girls and I had discussed at length Carlsbad Caverns—its origins and explanations—the entire road trip there.

I assumed Jack and Jo (seven and nine at the time) kinda knew what to expect in this adventure. I supposed they were as excited as I to see bats escape their caves *en masse*, stalagmites desperately reaching for the heavens, and stalactites searching for the entrance to hell.

We paid the park fee and followed the signs to the entrance of the caverns. We walked into the mouth of one, and that's when I heard Jo whisper in sheer wonderment, "Wow! And I thought this was gonna be boring..."

It made the whole trip worthwhile, dead man and all.

And you thought life was going to be boring.

Time Passages

Corridors

Fading down crooked halls of years

And cracked steps of days,

Leading to where?

~ age 16 (1978)

Russy Getted a Balloon Today

Russy getted a balloon today. From the doctor. It costed him nothing. He jes didn't yell or nothing when he getted a shot for the bee stings.

I never getted a balloon from Dr. Gee. I guess I shoulda yelled the first time he poked at me.

It's pink, but Russy likes it still. It ain't jes any ole balloon, neither. It floats. Not like the ones at Althea's birthday parties you gotta blow up yourself. It really floats. Russy says it's cuzza hot air. You gotta let your breath get really hot afore you blow it up. My air never gets hot enough cuz I never get 'em to float.

Dr. Gee must got a lotta hot air.

Russy said he heared 'bout this guy in Denmark who finded a note onna balloon from a kid. Denmark is far, far away.

Russy gets the bestest ideas.

He writed his name onna piece a paper. Then he writed more.

I wished I could write.

He telled me it was our address.

Russy's the smartestest. He goes to school 'cuz he's lots older, like two whole years.

I asted Russy if I could hold his balloon. Jes for a minute. I'd be really careful.

But Russy said, "No, you'll pop it."

I would not.

He wanted to climb up onna barn roof and let it go so it could fly farther'n Denmark.

The ladder wobbled and made my tummick woozy, but I followed him anyway.

At the top, my hands wouldn't lissen to my brain tellin 'em to LET GO. They wouldn't lissen to Russy tellin me to Let Go; he'd grab me and help me up. But my hands wouldn't do nothin. I heared marchin in my ears and I couldn't breathe right. Russy had a look on his face that told me I had better get offa that ladder and onna that roof!

My hands heared that and got moving.

I standed there right next to Russy onna barn roof.

I did it! I didn't fall.

See? I telled you I could do it.

The pink balloon floated onna string in Russy's hand.

"Here," he said, and handed me the string. "Don't let go."

"I won't. I ain't stupid, you know?"

He handed me the string!

I holded his pink balloon!

I wished he'd give it to me 'stead of the guy in Denmark. I bet that ole guy don't even like pink balloons. Yellow's my favorite color, but pink's good —for a balloon. Not for a dress, though. When I'm growed up, I'm gonna get wedded in a yellow dress the color of lemon pudding Mom makes onna stove. She lets me stir it and I like 'tending of a long, yellow dress the same silky color. When I'm all growed I won't gotta wear Russy's stinkin ole clothes no more.

Russy looked for the paper he writed on. I hoped he don't find it for a long time. I liked the way the wind blowed the balloon 'round onna string. That's jes how my long, yellow dress'll float 'crossa floor and —

"Sandy!"

"What?"

His face telled me he tried to get me to hear afore, but my brain was off floatin with the pink balloon.

"Give it back." His hand reached out for the string.

I holded it tight and thinked I might say, "No."

I looked around. We standed on the barn roof. No place to run. He'd catch me for sure if'n I tried. Prolly fall offa the roof—then we'd catch it from Poppa.

"Give it here." His face telled me he was really mad now.

I tried to hand it to him.

I holded out my fist.

I thought he had it.

I thought he took the string. I really did.

Why would I let go if I knowed he ain't getted it?

But nobody getted it, and his pink balloon getted away.

I tried to grab the string when I seed he ain't getted it, but I missed.

Russy's face telled me he knowed he shouldn'ta let me hold his balloon.

I wished he'd stop lookin at me that way.

"That guy in Denmark'll prolly getted it. It's floatin way high up," I telled him.

"Yeah, but now he won't know who it's from, stoop." He holded the paper in his fist and shaked it at me. His face telled me he might cry, but he quick goed down the ladder.

"Don't call me stupid. I ain't stupid, stupid. You's the one what let go. I handed it to you, Stupid." I followed him down the ladder. I tried hard not to cry, but I did anyway. I knowed it was all my fault. But I wished he wouldn't lookit me that way.

Next time I go to Dr. Gee's I won't yell or nothing and maybe he'll give me a floating balloon.

If he does, I'm givin it to Russy...even if it's yellow.

Then maybe he won't lookit me that way.

Mine!

At what age does one have permission to lay claim to their stuff? My eldest tells me she's currently fighting the "mine!" battle with her eldest, who is five. We (as parents) have all lived through that particularly wonderful struggle at one time or another, I'd wager. We all do our best to ensure our children are selfless and kind to others.

So at what age is it okay to possess your possessions?

I own things all the time. My refrigerator, my car's windshield, my children, my home, my brandy-like-new coffeepot.

My daughter Jack was upset the other day because Monster wanted to play on her scooter.

"Monster wants to ride my scooter."

Monster's mom (indignant at best) said, "Your scooter?" And she looked at me with *that* look.

You know the one. The one which states I've been remiss at raising an unselfish child. How dare Jack not share *her* stuff with Monster.

I asked Jack later why she didn't want to share. She said, "He breaks everything I own."

And he does. He breaks everything, even the unbreakable.

So why can't Jack be the ruler of her possessions? I am. I won't let anyone drive my car. I tell the little ones at home to stay out of my room and my stuff. I tell them, "If it ain't yours, don't touch it," and I refuse to share my dark chocolate with… okay, I share, but I let them know how privileged they are to be allowed to partake of my dark chocolate…just one.

When I was barely learning to play well with others and some kid took my favorite stuffed bear, my mother would've smacked me good if I'd put up a fuss and said, "Mine!" Yet, if someone nabbed her car, she'd be screaming for justice. (As we all would.)

Did she forget how to share?

Do we all forget how to share?

Why is it a toddler is expected to give freely of his or her belongings and yet we, as adults, are not? When did we pass the "mine!" mile marker? At what age? Did I miss the rite of passage associated with said privilege?

Mine.

This is mine. I have a right to it, because it's mine.

As I walked through a parking lot quite a few years ago with my eldest three at my side, I wondered at what age I stopped holding their hands to cross busy streets and parking lots. When was the magical moment I decided my children were old enough. Or had I just stopped obsessing?

So much of life is marked by telltale signs of resignation. Or is it maturation? I don't know which. Why do we not see these signs for what they are? Why are we blind to subtle changes which really aren't subtle at all, in retrospect?

It's Jack's scooter. She ought to have a right to allow whomever she wants to ride it, or not ride it, as the case may be. She ought to wield that power over her life. So much of the power in her life is held by others. So what if Monster doesn't get his way this time? There'll be other days he can break her scooter.

Maybe it's time to re-think the whole "mine" issue and let the kids have a say in their lives. You wouldn't be so hip on sharing your stuff with *your* neighbors, would you?

Hey, by the way, can I play with your...

I Amn't Kidding

On Thursday night Jo had a concert at school. During the concert, her music teacher reminded the parents in the audience there would be a party Friday morning for our kids and to *not forget* the treat our child promised to bring...

Huh? Treat? We don't need no stinkin' treat. Of what treat does she speak? And she needs it when?

I'm sure as parents, you, too, have had the sinking 'deer out of water' feeling at least once regarding school.

"Oh, yeah, Mom. I forgot to tell you. I'm supposed to bring donuts tomorrow morning." (For thirty-seven kids and two adults, I might add.)

So needless to say (but I'm going to say it anyway) we headed to the store directly after the concert. We hurried through the aisles and toward the donut section, mother followed by two children—lagging behind, which was par.

As she passed the candy aisle, Jack picked up a push-pop candy on steroids. It had a trigger action which allowed its owner to push up his or her flavor of choice—it offered five choice flavors.

Where else in life does one get five choices? On demand? With a flip of a switch?

"Mom, can I have this?"

"Only if I can hit you," I said, and hurried on my quest for doughy nuts.

I didn't halt, nor did I slow, but I threw a glance over my shoulder. I was certain she'd understood my quip as a solid

"No," but much to my dismay Jack continued on behind me, push-pop in hand.

I walked backwards, face toward her.

"Jack. Put that back!"

"It's okay," she said, with a determined look on her face. "You can hit me."

I thought I was going to pee myself.

She'd weighed her options and reconciled with the consequences.

Besides, she knew I hit like a girl.

Yeah, I bought it for her—reimbursing her for the good laugh. And no, I didn't hit her. But I reserve the right to in the future.

A Cavemom Can Do It

I look around my house and see piles of crap doing what they're wont to do: piling up. Have you noticed nothing ever piles down... except for maybe stalactites.

Anyway, I asked the girls the other day, for the umpteenth time, to *please* pick up after themselves.

I swear! These Neanderthals I call my children have their father's disease. I'll give it a name... wait for it.

Let's call it the "goo-D-nuf" disease.

The goo-D-nuf disease. You know, they put the dirty dishes *next to* the dishwasher, or *next to* the sink, never in either one (if they bother bringing their dirty dishes back to the kitchen at all, that is).

They put their dirty clothes (*if* they take them from the middle of their bedroom floor) *next to* the closed laundry room door. When they put their clean, folded clothes away, they only make as far as *next to* their closet or their dresser.

They put their trash *next to* the trash can, either on the floor or on the neighboring counter (if they bother to bring it in from the surfaces throughout the house which surround our lives).

And all this they declare is goo-D-nuf!

Seriously? You already brought it most of the way. Finish the job, for goodness sake! How hard is it to actually put something where it belongs?

Recently I told Jo and Jack I wished they'd let me know

who and where the maid was, because I needed to fire her; she was failing at her job.

"In fact," I pondered aloud to them, "I doubt she even exists as I don't remember hiring her... and I've never seen her."

Jo said, "That's because you never look in the mirror. I know this because your hair needs combed... badly!"

"Oh, yeah? Well, sweetheart (and I use the term lightly), if I didn't have to keep picking up after Neanderthals with goo-D-nuf disease, I might have more time to work on my hair. Besides, my hair is already combed badly, thank you very much."

How hard can it be? *It's so easy...*

Time to Soak It All In

In Greek mythology (and other spiritual memes) water is the element of emotion. Maybe that's why after a hard, exceptionally emotional day I find myself longing for the comfort of a soak in my uncomfortably small bathtub.

Seriously? Why do they make small bathtubs, anyway? It seems a waste of time and materials to me. I'd imagine even tiny people (children) like to immerse themselves in hot, soothing water 'way past their ears. I know I do. Or would like to, anyway.

So picture this... well, all but the me-being-naked part, please:

I draw a bath, grab a glass of wine and a good book, and start to slip into the warm blanket of tangible emotion... until the slipping comes to a screeching halt as my feet hit the opposite side of the tub and my arse barely makes the cut. And I'm short. So I'm just saying—the tub is small, really small.

I turn off the water, because the two-bucket tub is already filled to the brim, and soak my bottom half.

A sip of wine and a crack-open of the book later, I find myself shivering, as my ceramic-coated-metal, too-small tub has effectively shortened the lifespan of the hot factor of the bath water in record time.

At this point, I'm sure tree-huggers hate my stress-reducing ritual.

I drain the tub a bit, and then add more water—straight

hot this time—until it starts to turn tepid from the spout (I have water heater issues, too). I put down my book and wine glass, and sticking my feet in the air, I soak my top half—head and all. As the warm, fuzzy water enters my ear canals and reverberates the creaks, bangs, and other sounds of (apparently) my home's digestive system, I relax and ponder the events of the day. My mind wanders, and I wonder...

I wonder if Ted Bundy knew Ann Rule, his co-worker, had a penchant for writing and that his life would soon be on display in a loverly little book of hers, *The Stranger Beside Me*. I wonder if he would've treated her any differently had he known.

I wonder why some of the people I've met recently look and act a lot like Andrea Yates.

I wonder if something in the water in this little town makes almost every woman I've met (who's lived here all her life) want to *not* cut her hair...ever... or desperately attempt to keep the spiral perm of the 1980s perpetually in style by donning it for decades. And I wonder why most of these women seem to be so obtuse.

I know they watch TV... well, at least the important shows like *Dancing with the Next American Idol*, and *The Last Surviving Bachelor*. They ought to at least be somewhat fashion-savvy.

And I wonder if there's a book in all that wondering for me to write.

With little exception (unless I'm alone in my home) I am reminded to wonder why sitting in a tepid tub, soaking away the effects of the day is call for little ones to barge in and ask such inane questions as "What are you doing?" or say grating things like "She won't let me watch what I want to watch."

And I wonder why, when they soak, they inevitably scream from what should be the calm interior of the bathroom, "Mawm!" And, upon entering the bathroom, I most often hear phrases like "Can you hand me the soap?' or "Please turn off the water."

Why is that, I wonder?

I wonder if bubbles really are tiny universes full of little worlds and other lives which exist for their own definition of eternity while the fragile emotional orb remains intact—a belief I've held tightly in my mind's grasp since I first discovered the concept at the age of three. With that thought in mind, I wonder if creating the bubbles and then popping them makes me a god or a demon.

I sit up, drain the tub, refill it—using the aforementioned steps for which conservationists despise people like me. Lather, rinse, repeat.

And then I wonder what it's all about, Alfie. I wonder why people treat people the way they do. Why men cheat, why women bitch, why kids are abused and neglected.

And then I think, *You know, if I had a hot tub my kids would be hot-tub orphans.*

Heck, even if I had a tad larger tub they'd be pseudo-neglected.

Maybe that's why they make too-small tubs.

For mothers like me.

I wonder...

Keeping It In Perspective

Yesterday after school Jo came stomping through the front room door, tossed down her book bag, and shouted to the ceiling:

"Today is the worst day of my life ever!"

Then she stopped in mid-fit, looked at me with a quiet, strange expression, and added, "Besides the day I die."

Keep it in perspective, people.

Some Facts of Life

When living with girls, especially a lot of girls (which I've done for the past twenty-plus years) one must keep in mind these little facts of life:

1. You'll go through tons of toilet paper. It's a fact of life. Girls wipe every time they go potty, regardless. But thank God they do, because if they didn't it would increase the...

2. Piles of clothing! Clean clothing and clothes that need to be washed. Girls change their clothes at least twice a day. The laundry pile heaps with tried-on-but-not-worns. Most of the time this happens because their outfit doesn't quite match their...

3. Shoes! Tons and tons of shoes everywhere. In the hall. Under the table. Near the couch. But always underfoot. Not the type of "under foot" for which they're designed, of course. More often than not, though, the perfect pair for their current outfit is lost within the confines of their...

4. Ever-messy bedroom! I mean, really? It's a frickin' disaster-area. How can they walk in there without stepping on anything and breaking their foot or their something? Not only piles of aforementioned clothing, but stacks of...

5. Dirty dishes and used glasses! Come on, kids. Is it truly *that* difficult to bring your used kitchenware back to the kitchen? And once there, is it really a feat to put the dirty stuff in the dishwasher instead of the counter next to it? And how about the...

6. Heaps of trash! Gum wrappers, pop-tart foils, straws—

the list never ends—piled everywhere. Even on the desk or counter next to their trash can. Seriously? Come on, you guys. You're beginning to act a lot like your father, whose parents, I believe, excused his sloppiness and poor hygiene on the old adage "Boys will be..."

7. Boys! Calling on the phone. Knocking at our door. Tearing up my fence. Breaking anything and everything they can get their hands on. And sticking around until meal time so they, too, can...

8. Eat me out of house and home! Ohmigod, these girls can't stop eating. Especially the little one. At least she sticks mainly to good food like grapes, apples, and cheese sticks, but damn! It sure does make for...

9. Skyrocketing bills! Leaving the faucet on, taking more than one shower a day, leaving the television and lights on when they're not even in the house. I even have to remind them nightly to turn out the bathroom light when they come to give me their good-night...

10. Kisses and hugs! And plenty of 'em... which renders the other nine items insignificant.

Interruptions

Ring telephone, ring tonight,

Ding-a-ling with all your might.

Many times a welcomed noise,

Often from the girls and boys,

Who call on me to make the scene,

After pulling on my faded jeans.

But not now you wretched thing.

My heart cries out to stop that ring!

I know your style to ne'er quit,

Until I've up and answered it.

But please! I beg of you to stop!

I do wish you were better taught.

You scream at me with fierce annoy,

I do believe, to you, a joy.

Still my brains are scrambled pegs,

Like this morn's half-eaten eggs.

I hear you as I rack my brain,

And try to ponder something sane.

But still you ring and ring some more,

My prayers and pleas you so ignore.

I beg of you, you nasty thing,

Please think of something else to sing,

While I ponder, gaze, and wonder,

At the paper through which I blunder,

To have complete by dawn of light.

So ring, telephone, ring tonight.

~ age 14 (1976)

That Socks

I hate folding socks.

If I had a million dollars, I'd pay someone to match, fold, and put away the socks of this household.

I cannot remember a time when I didn't have a laundry basket full of socks awaiting a gentle hand to sort and pair them like a love-match website for foot mittens. Maybe when I was two and the sock-folding task belonged to my mother.

I sit here—right now—looking at the seemingly insurmountable pile of socks in the white wicker laundry basket on my dining room floor.

I put them there so I can be reminded I have yet one more household task to complete before I can relax. Doesn't work. It only reminds me how much I hate to fold socks. And as I've already revealed, I'm sitting on my ass... er...my living room couch.

Do you know how many socks a household of six females can accumulate? Sure, there are only three at home now, but it doesn't make it any less depressing, or the pile any less formidable.

Yes, I could have my eight-year-old and ten-year-old fold their own dang socks, but then I'd still have to do mine. And why give the task I hate most in the world to tiny people? What kind of person would that make me?

Besides, if I did that I wouldn't have anything to bitch about today.

And they'd mismatch most of them anyway. They don't

care if one is lemon meringue yellow and another one is sunlight yellow. Hey, two yellow socks—BINGO! Too bad the lengths don't match up and one's stripes are a different shade of blue than the other's green polka-dots.

Seriously. Do you think anyone would take a job to come into my house, maybe once a week, to fold our socks? I don't want a maid. I don't mind cleaning my own house because it's small and I know it's clean when I clean it. But if I were rich enough I might rethink having a maid...and a cook... and a cabana boy.

"Oh, cabana boy. *Una más cerveza, por favor...*"

Meanwhile, I'd sit in my bathhouse, soaking my woes away.

Is there anybody out there with a sock fetish who would love to come to my house and help me out? How much would one charge for that? As my sister would say, "How many nickels you got?"

Is there a website for odd jobs like that? Well, there should be. For instance, I could register as a towel folder, because folding towels is almost therapeutic.

I wouldn't mind unloading a dishwasher, but I really don't like loading one.

I could separate your laundry and start your washer, but you'd have to do the rest.

I'd do your chores palatable to me, and in turn you'd do my chores that bring me down.

Not that I have a household chore fetish, by any means. Truth be told, I could be a woman of leisure. If you wanted to do all of my household chores—hey, who am I to deny you?

I'm accepting applications immediately.

Apply within.

And Nothing But

I find these truths to be self-evident:

1. The pizza won't cook unless and until you actually put it inside the oven. All the pre-heating aside, eventually you have to remember to put it in there.

2. The pizza burns if you forget to remove it from the oven. I promise.

3. Kids won't eat burnt pizza …unless you tell them they can't. So tell them they can't, already. Problem solved.

4. No matter how many times you tell them, your kids forget how to put a new roll on the toilet paper dispenser or how much toilet paper is 'enough' already.

5. The phone always rings—or your nosy neighbor walks right in—the second you sit down on the toilet or step into the bathtub. Unless, of course, you plan ahead and take the phone with you and lock the front door beforehand.

6. The one day you plan an unbelievably fun activity for yourself (outside the realm of being a mom), school closes or goes on delayed start due to nasty weather, or your child wakes up with a fever.

7. The paint, nail polish, varnish, or glue won't dry unless or until you touch it to see if it's dried yet, only to leave a nice smear or fingerprint. And you'll never be able to convince your children to *not* test this theory.

8. No matter what you do for your adult children and no matter how much money you've already given them for rent, car payment, or college, they'll never remember not paying

you back and insist it was their sister, not they, who borrowed last time. Because of this, they'll likely say, "And can you please lend me some money since you always lend her some," in their best "you've always loved her more" kind of way. (Don't worry, you'll get payback when your grandchildren borrow from them and forget all about it.) If you offer viable proof of said loan, you'll undoubtedly get the "Do you have to remind me and make me feel like crap when I'm already stressed enough?" speech.

9. No matter what kind of mother you are, you will *always* be blamed for your children's woes and hardships. They all end up in some kind of counseling session complaining of your lacks and mistakes. I guarantee if Mother Theresa had a daughter, she'd end up in counseling, too. Make no mistake about it. So you may as well suck at being a mom, because you're going to be blamed for everything anyway.

10. No matter what you teach your children about the evils of cigarettes and drugs and alcohol, they'll listen to their friends more. If their friends are into it, they will be, too. You can only hope they come out of the "stupid tunnel" before the light at the end of it turns out to be an oncoming, fast-moving train. Repeat after me: This, too, shall pass.

11. The exact moment you shampoo the carpet or mop the floor, little Susie (or one of her friends) will have fumble-finger disease and spill her cherry Kool-Aid. But she won't merely spill it. Oh, no. She'll actually try to catch the falling cup (bless her heart) and instead catapult the cup to the wall, successfully spreading the red, sticky mess from wall to wall and halfway up.

12. There are more truths, but the truth is my meno-pause-al brain forgot the rest. Thanks for playing.

Reflections

Who is in the mirror

Gazing back at you?

You thought you could be one,

And still be part of two.

But, time holds no man's hand,

And luck is a passing thing.

Hold on to ones you love,

Hold fast to songs you sing.

For happiness is for those who make it,

Loneliness is all it seems.

You get what you put into love

And how much you believe in dreams

~ age 16 (1978)

The "Every Other" Parent

A close acquaintance recently went through some child support and visitation issues with the father of her two-year-old child.

She relayed the compromises she's had to make and the added benefits he receives for the child he denied having, until the DNA tests proved him—and his mother—wrong.

It got me thinking as she stated now that he knows the child is his, he wants her child every other Thanksgiving, every other Christmas, and a month every summer. But he balks at paying her any kind of child support or back-support for this child.

Why do so many non-custodial parents want to be the Disneyland Parent but don't like the money aspect of child support? They want to buy the ice cream and visit all the area attractions and show their children "a really good time" the entire twenty days of their yearly parental participation. But to hell with their offspring the other 345 days per year. Meanwhile, the custodial parent has to spend all of their income on rent, insurance, medicine, child care, car, utilities, clothing, food, school supplies, and fund raisers. We don't have extras for fun stuff, exciting places, or ice cream. How dare we ask for any kind of monetary support?

A truly fair sharing of parental responsibilities and visitation would be listed more like this:

You get them every other flu or cold ailment.

You get them every other routine doctor visit.

You get them every other serious illness, injury, or surgery.

You get them every other braces realignment and dentist appointment.

You get them every other conniption fit, shouting match, and meltdown.

You get them every other parent-teacher conference or PTO meeting.

You get them every other sibling rivalry dispute over the stupid little plastic made-in-China toy you gave them last Christmas when you didn't have them.

Every other time the school calls and our child needs to be picked up, you get to explain to your boss, take the time off from work, and pick up our child from school or daycare and take them to the doctor for meds—and you get to stay up with them all night, cleaning up their puke and poop and snot. You get to try to bring the fever down, and you get to worry if you can't.

Every other time the school has an awards ceremony, you get to attend the entire two-hour program to watch our child for the two seconds they're on stage.

Every other time the school calls with disciplinary or education problems, you get to talk to the principal or teacher or nurse, or parent of the other child.

You get to nag at our children to clean their rooms every other time it's needed.

Every other day you get to ensure our children brush their teeth and hair, take a shower, wash behind their ears, and put their dirty clothes in the wash.

And every other week you get to do their laundry.

You get to hear them complain every other time they're told to turn off the TV and do their homework.

You get to deal with the school bully every other time our child is tormented.

You get to hear our child every other time they say the world isn't fair.

Every other time they ask if they can go to the movies or out to dinner, you get to tell them we don't have the money for it.

You get to hold them every other time their best friend breaks their heart, and you get to be the one who tells them "this too shall pass" and "if they can't see what a wonderful person you are, they don't deserve you."

And you get to wait and worry every other time they're twenty minutes late or don't answer their phone.

Every other time someone invites you out for one thing or another, you get to decline because you can't find (or afford) a decent babysitter.

And every other time someone invites me out for one thing or another, you get to find and pay for a babysitter so I *can* go out.

Noncustodial parents want the December 25ths and fourth Thursdays of November. We get to have them the 21st of April.

You're right. That's not any special day.

But what we know and the noncustodial parent doesn't is this: The date doesn't matter—Christmas, Thanksgiving or April 21st. Any day spent with our child—this wonderful soul—is Thanksgiving. And every morning kiss is a Christmas present.

Noncustodial Disneyland Parents will never figure that one out, will they?

Same

Time flies,

Eyes dry,

And we still can't stand the pain.

He lies,

I cry,

And we still can't seem to change.

~ age 17 (1979)

There's Nothing Good About It

I used to know a woman who was nervous around microwave ovens. It seems she believed they were harmful to your health and would eventually cause cancer if you stood near one or consumed the food heated in it. She believed the waves were bad for your heart.

Those fears were unfounded—for her anyway.

She ought to have feared her son instead of the microwave.

She died on her front lawn from a gunshot wound to the heart—inflicted by her twenty-three-year-old son, who subsequently turned the gun on himself.

When we first decide to have children, we have aspirations for them—none of which include drugs or violence. We hold our infant child, no larger than our arms can handle, and whisper to her our hopes and dreams. We watch with adoring eyes as she grows, and we reach out to catch her when she takes her first tumble while learning to walk... and for a while wonder if she'll be able to take more than a few steps before kissing the carpet again. But she masters the art, and soon we're chasing her around the house.

I've heard women say they want a child for the unconditional love between mother and child.

Newsflash: That whole unconditional love thing on your child's part lasts about two years, if you're lucky. Then your adorable child does the unthinkable. She starts to develop a personality of her own. She wants to feed herself in the highchair, even though more makes it onto the floor than into her belly. She doesn't want to wear that beautiful dress you bought, because the lace itches. She doesn't like the gym shoes you picked out, because her nemesis in junior high gym class wears the exact same pair.

Then comes high school and the fights begin. The "I hate you"s and the rolling of the eyes. You think it, too, but you'd never say it to your child. Instead you say, "I love you, but I do *not* love your behavior."

She throws a dirty shirt at you, grunts something unintelligible, and slams her bedroom door in your face.

And you sit quietly on your couch, remembering her little hand in yours, the way she looked up at you with total trust and commitment, her little voice saying, "I love you momma. I want to live with you forever."

Then you hear her scream from inside her room, "I can't wait to get away from you and to move out of this house!"

And you wonder what you did to change this angel into a devil in a mere matter of months. You wonder why you were unable to better show your love for her. You wonder if it will ever be good between you two again.

But it will.

And it does get better. She calls you from her apartment or dorm and talks to you about her heartaches, sister problems, and money woes. You help her out when you can, but you feel like it's never enough because you sense her growing up —and growing away from you every day. You see her becoming more a woman and less your little girl.

And then she really does leave. You find yourself standing on the front porch, watching her drive away. And you know you may never see her again because she's moving to the other side of the country. And your heart breaks once more. The tears flow.

Not for the first time, you wish you could have done more to connect with her.

You hope she knows how much you love her, how much her presence enhanced your life.

You wave good-bye and you let her go.

Circular

People,

sitting,

talking

Self-indulgent;

In thoughts of themselves,

Tearing long painted nails

Into the baby faces

Of others

(like them)

Smearing the blood

In familiar patterns.

~ age 17 (1979)

It's Time for You to Go

We've been down this road before, but it seems to me we need a refresher course, so we're going to play a little game.

Read this phrase:

"It's time for you to go."

Did you read it?

Question is, how did you read it?

Picture a young mother lost in thought. She looks up at the clock and sees the time. "Oh my! How late it is. William, it's time for you to go. You're gonna miss the bus again."

Picture a young wife, midsection bursting with a child inside, standing beside her young husband in uniform. She looks over his shoulder and sees his company filing single file onto the waiting bus.

"William," she says. "We'll be all right, don't you worry. I'll send word when the baby comes. I have so much I want to say... so much more to tell you, but... it's time for you to go. I love you, William." She fights off the urge to cry, blinks away the oncoming tears and kisses him good-bye, knowing it may be the last kiss between them. "Be safe," she says.

Picture a woman in ragged clothing on her knees, washing down the worn floor with a soiled cloth. She brushes her loose, sweaty bangs from her eyes and sighs deeply. She eyes the bloodstain she's been straining to clean and starts scrubbing once more. She speaks to the floor with labored and deliberate speech, one word per scrub. "You are the only evidence left of William, that no-good beatin' cheatin' bastard. You've put up quite a fight. But now, dear blood, it's time for you to go."

Picture an older, affluent woman with her hand on her hip. Her other hand clutches the front door knob. The door is opened wide. The stately, refined woman is clearly ticked. Facing her, a young man holds pictures of her husband in a compromising position with the young man's wife, Monica. The man smiles and says, "We're both reasonable adults here. Clearly you wouldn't want your husband's good name tarnished, would you? Not with the upcoming election. What do you think his constituents would say if they saw these pictures, say, on the front page of tomorrow's Times? I believe, Mrs. Clinton, we could come to some sort of financial agreement—"

"And I believe, sir, it's time for you to go," she says.

Picture a man, standing in his wife's closet among her designer dresses and expensive pumps. In one shaking hand he grips a love letter to her from his best friend. In the other, a gun. His wife stands behind him, her face riddled with guilt, shame, fear, and defiance. Without turning to face her he says, defeated, "I think... it's time for you to go."

She steps forward, hand out and says, "But William... please... let me expl—"

"I SAID IT'S TIME FOR YOU TO GO!"

Picture a woman seated in a chair beside a hospital bed. She's on death watch. She looks at her brother's badly beaten face, and the tubes and wires keeping him tied to this world. "Oh, William," she says to the comatose man. "Who did this to you?"

"I'm really, truly sorry, Miss. But..."

She looks up to see the young nurse standing in her brother's hospital room doorway. "Yes?"

"Visiting hour is over, miss. It's time for you to go."

I've said it before and I'll say it again. The tone you put to a written word when you read it is your choice and your choice alone. You bring in your own perceptions, your ideals, your prejudices. And you decide what I'm saying by how you choose me to be saying it. You decide by coming to your own conclusions without any real evidence of who I am and what I meant by that.

I'm like your puppet in a way. If you want to laugh, my words will make you chuckle. But if you want to be angry, my words will make you mad.

More's the pity.

But now... it's time for me to go... fix dinner.

Thanks for playing.

Class Clowns

Class clowns

Funny frowns

Even when no one else

Is around.

We keep it up

And never cry

Over

Lost loves

Because

We're the

Class clowns.

~ age 16 (1978)

The Birthday Wish

"Are you sure you want to do this?"

"Yes, I've thought about it long and hard, young man. It's the right thing to do." She opened the small drawer on the end-table next to the chair in which she sat and pulled out an envelope. "Five million dollars, cashier's check made out to no one, as discussed. I'm trusting you to get the job done in a timely manner. I want to be alive to see what my money can buy."

"Right thing to do? I've never heard it put that way before, but if you're sure." The man folded the envelope and placed it in his inside jacket pocket. He looked hard at the ancient lady, noticing the string of pearls hanging from her frail neck. "You've paid the money. Every thing's in order. Just…"

"Just what? You think I'm crazy, don't you? So do my children, so that's nothing new up my skirt." Her bright, watery eyes flashed at him.

"You told your children what you're wanting me to do?" Alarm flashed through his heart. That could be a deal breaker. The less anyone knew, the better.

"Heavens no, child. They think I'm crazy in general." The woman's laughter tinkled throughout her front room. It seemed to cascade off the crystal chandelier and back onto the beveled glass of the massive bay windows of the sitting room.

I'm beginning to agree with them, the man thought.

"I have to ask you…why?" He stared at her, wanting to understand. He'd been in this situation many times before.

It was his occupation, his life. But why her? Why this old silver-haired lady who seemed to have everything? She had all the money in the world. Obviously, she could afford it. And he'd been lucky so far, but luck isn't guaranteed and the prospect of getting caught...well, he didn't want to think about it.

"You didn't ask my name," she said, changing the subject.

"I don't need to. I investigated you before I took on this job," he said. "I know your name is JoAnna, and you're seventy-nine years old—

"Eighty, next week," JoAnna interrupted, and winked.

He smiled. "I know your husband of fifty-nine years died eleven months ago of a heart attack, just days before your sixtieth wedding anniversary. I know you have five children, seven grandchildren and you've had a fairly easy life, with the exception of a baby who died at six months of age, and a grandson who died in the war last year.

"You were the president of the Woman's Humane Society for many years, and you and your husband contributed much to various worthy causes. You championed for the abolition of the death penalty and are outspoken against abortions for any reason. And you've not missed a day of church, except once when you were giving birth to your third child, which is why I'm having a hard time understanding your decision."

"Don't fret it, Joe. Someday you'll understand." She winked again. "So the price is one thousand dollars per and another fifty million when the job is complete, payable on proof, correct?"

"Yeah, that's the contract, but—"

"Don't call me a butt." Tinklings of laughter again cascaded from JoAnna's glowing face. Her eyes lit up and he couldn't help smiling at her. "My children always used to say that. Oh, how they loved to tease each other. Such a kinder world, then." Her eyes went vacant and a Mona Lisa smile played on her face, as if thinking of that kinder world. She snapped back to reality with a little, almost audible, pop. "Would you like some more tea?" Her hand went up in the air. A woman in a black uniform appeared at her side, as if by magic.

"Uh, no, thank you. But I'd love a Scotch…on the rocks, if you have it."

JoAnna's smile disappeared. "We usually don't drink in this house. Such a nasty habit."

He felt his face grow hot. Here he was, a thirty-two-year-old trained assassin, ashamed for asking for a drink in the afternoon, especially considering the topic of conversation. "Oh, I apologize. Tea would be fine, thank you."

JoAnna's smile reappeared. "Champagne, then. To celebrate. Nancy, bring us our best bottle and two glasses. We're going to celebrate the birthday present Joe is giving me."

"Champagne it is," he said, and forced a smile. He wished she'd stop calling him Joe. But then, what else should she call him? He didn't and wouldn't give his real name, not to anyone. Especially in his line of work.

He waited until Nancy had left the room.

"One thousand dollars a head. As requested. But I assume you want proof," he said.

JoAnna sat up a bit. "Why, video of course. How else would I be able to keep count? The entire ruckus will probably be too much for y'all to keep tally. Let me. I'll give a bonus of ten thousand dollars cash for every fifty, just in case I miss a few. I'll add it to the final payout. We can record the kills so we can review them when you pick up your final check—just to be sure I don't cheat you inadvertently."

"Video? Are you sure you want to see that?"

"Oh, Joe, nothing bothers me anymore. Besides, it'll be nice to know the job is getting done right. I don't think I could leave this world in such a mess. I need to do my part before I go. Such a shame." JoAnna's eyes watered and a tear coursed down her cheek. She wiped it away. "When I was a little girl, Grandpappy sat me on his knee and told me I'd not succeed in life unless I left this world a better place than I found it. He died soon after, but his words stayed with me.

"When my grandson Jonah died last year, it nearly broke my daughter's heart. She hasn't been the same since. She takes comfort in the fact he was making life better for others in another country. He did his civic duty. He died a hero."

JoAnna straightened her spine and sat up a bit in her chair. She continued with clarity and strength. "When I heard on the news that over three thousand American soldiers had died in the Mid-East wars, I didn't think my heart could take it…the pain of knowing what those other families are going through. Then later in the same newscast, they reported more than a hundred thousand innocent people have been murdered on American soil since the war began. Well, I thought, how incredible! People are outraged that our children are dying in war but have no emotion that over thirty times the amount of senseless murders are taking place in our own country, mostly by gang members and hoodlums. And it's only getting worse."

JoAnna looked down at her wrinkled, gnarled hands and quietly shook her head.

"If the local and state governments can't or won't do anything to help honest citizens, I can. And I will." She looked up with an intensity he had rarely seen. "Yes. Video. Livestream video. Kill all the bastards you can find. Anyone you see committing a crime. Anyone with a gang-related tattoo—I don't care the age or sex. Get rid of them. And don't fuck with me here. I know I'm an old lady, but I found you and I can find someone else to get rid of you if you betray me in any way."

They sat, eye-locked for what seemed an eternity.

"You have my word, JoAnna."

"Good. They have the technology for livestream video, right?"

"Yes'm"

"Good. Get your men over here to set up a room for screens and such, or whatever. Then we'll move on to the next step, the real reason you're here. Hire enough of you ex-Delta-force types you need to cover the United States. Start here on the East Coast. Sweep from north to south, beginning with the big cities. You can come back for the smaller towns if need be. We'll call it Operation Clean Sweep."

JoAnna's face lit up with a bright smile, as if quite pleased with herself.

Nancy appeared with glasses and champagne. The room grew silent as she poured.

"To your birthday, JoAnna." He raised his glass in salute.

"To my birthday. And to Operation Clean Sweep."

American Soil-ed

I'm feeling a little saddened today. If you can't tell by my ramblings I hold a soft spot in my heart for soldiers.

Could someone please explain the logic behind the media propaganda against the United States' assistance in Iraq?

Lately I've been hearing the term *Iraqi Invasion* everywhere, from my mom's friends to the talking heads on TV. I find that terminology rude and insulting. It's a personal issue. You don't need to agree.

Invasion: entrance of an army to conquer or pillage.

So... are our troops conquering or pillaging over there? Do they take turns? Pillaging on Monday, Wednesday, and Friday with conquering limited to Tuesday, Thursday, and Saturday? Keeps everyone on track, and apparently everyone gets Sunday off to watch football?

Since the beginning of the war, websites have sprung up naming, claiming, and blaming the deaths of our soldiers in combat. The latest numbers (as of this posting) according to www.antiwar.com/casualities from 19 March 2003 (beginning of mission) to 20 October 2007 show 3,149 United States soldiers have died in combat in Iraq. They're passing around petitions for everyone to sign. They want the "senseless" deaths to stop. I don't blame them.

More than three thousand soldiers. That's tragic.

My heart goes out to the families and friends of the fallen.

I don't mean to belittle or trivialize their sacrifice in any way or by any amount. It's heartbreaking.

Let's look at some different numbers and you try to tell me what they mean.

3,023 people

2,865 people

What do these numbers represent?

It's the number of people who have been killed in certain places since the beginning of our mission in Iraq. Do you have a guess as to where?

No idea?

Okay, I'll tell you.

3,023 people have been murdered in New York City (not including suburbs and outlying areas) since the beginning of the mission in Iraq (March 2003) until present.

2,865 people have been murdered in Chicago (not including suburbs and outlying areas) since the beginning of the mission in Iraq (March 2003) until present.

Five thousand eight hundred, eighty-eight.

5,888

5,888 murders from 2003-07 in *two* American cities. *Two* cities have almost double the number of killings within the same time period. The tragedy here is there isn't a war in Chicago or New York City—as far as I know. But nearly 6,000 people have been killed anyway.

I don't see anyone putting a ticker on killings within the city limits of Chicago or New York. I don't see any outrage on the faces of the talking heads.

I wonder how much higher that number would be if you added up all of the murders from Hawaii to Maine, Alaska to Alabama—front to side, top to bottom.

Let's see, shall we?

According to the Disaster Center Website:

17,034 murders occurred in the US in 2006.

16,704 in 2005.

16,148 in 2004.

16,528 in 2003.

They don't have final numbers for 2007, but if I were to average this out from the numbers they provide, I come up with approximately 17,000 murders in 2007.

83,018 people murdered on American soil from 2003 to 2007.

I, too, want the senseless deaths to stop. Where's that damned petition?

(Pssst...This is where you look the other way.)

Dear Mr. Stephen King,

First, I hope you and Tabitha are well. Forgive my intrusion into your life, but I have some questions regarding publishers. I considered mailing this to your home, but concluded the chances of you getting it are as remote as you reading my blog.

So...when you were an up-and-coming writer, did you have to submit the first chapter of *Carrie* or *The Shining* on bright white paper, double-spaced with one-inch borders, with your name and title of the book in the header, along with the page number? Were you required to use only Times Roman or Courier font at ten to twelve points?

Did you have to write a catchy, all-consuming synopsis of the story for the remaining chapters of your book which (amazingly) fit on one page? Were you also required to place in one cover sheet your accolades, your education, the reason why you wrote the book, why you think there's a need for said book, how many other books like yours are out there, why yours is different, and how much you'd be willing to kiss the ass of the publisher if they took your book seriously?

And then, after winning The Dixie Lee Connor Award for the best Children's or Young Adult Manuscript at the 2005 Harriette Austin Writers Conference in Atlanta, Georgia, and an agent swooped in to represent you, did that same agent rape your words and make you change your story/story line no less than forty times before Editor Anne of Random House Children's Books got so fed up with the antics she threw in

the towel and you found yourself adrift on a desert island...
again. Without a publisher and without an agent?

Oh, wait, that was me...

I've considered getting on stage, wearing a cone bra
and gyrating to songs professing my virginity, becoming
famous for my boobs, then writing a children's book (after
my SEX book goes national) ...maybe then the publishers
would notice me?

Unfortunately, I sing as well as Madonna writes.

I've been picked up for seven of my children's books by
an independent publisher, but I'm beginning to wonder if I'm
doing this correctly. I'm a babe in this ink-eat-page world,
and although it may sound as if I am bitter, I'm not. Just in
need of some guidance and the knowledge I'm not alone in
this writing world.

I'm sure you've gone through all this. I recall hearing you
speak at the Children's Literacy Center's sponsored reading
of *Insomnia* in Colorado Springs. You said you covered your
wall with rejection slips. I know exactly how you feel. I hear
Dr. Seuss was rejected numerous times before he was picked
up by a publisher, and that knowledge gave me hope until
I heard (don't know if it's true) he only got published after
he took the job of editor in said publishing house and published his own books. Then, of course, there's JK Rowling's
story, which gives hope as well... like a band-aid applied to
a severed arm.

Oh well, I don't think you can help me, but it's been
cathartic writing it all down. Thank you for your time. You're
one of my favorite travel agents. I appreciate your skill and
talent for transporting me to another place, another time, and
a different life with the stroke of your pen. Maybe someday
I can return the favor.

Thank you again,
Constant Reader

Rejected…but at Least I Tried

The first annual Novel Approach Short Story Contest left me with two gold star certificates for participation, and if you know anything about me and obligatory gold stars…

But seriously, it was fun playing. I enjoyed creating the two following short stories: *Best Laid Plans* and *Broken*, observing these guidelines:

WRITE A PIECE OF BETWEEN 1,000 AND 1,500 WORDS IN LENGTH. THE ONLY RULE IS IT MUST USE BOTH OF THE FOLLOWING SENTENCES:

1. THE LAND FELL AWAY FROM THE ROAD, LEADING TO A ROW OF ELM TREES, BEYOND WHICH LAY THE UNKNOWN.

2. HE (OR SHE) HELD IT IN ONE HAND AND REFLECTED ON THE SHOCKING SPEED AT WHICH HIS (OR HER) FORTUNES HAD TURNED AROUND, A LONGED-FOR MOMENT THAT, EVEN AS IT REGISTERED ON HIM (OR HER), CEASED TO BE A GOAL AND BECAME A MEMORY.

Best Laid Plans

"HE HELD IT IN ONE HAND," Enigami read, "AND REFLECTED ON THE SHOCKING SPEED AT WHICH HIS FORTUNES HAD TURNED AROUND, A LONGED-FOR MOMENT THAT, EVEN AS IT REGISTERED ON HIM, CEASED TO BE A GOAL AND BECAME A MEMORY."

Enigami closed the book's cover and slumped down on its edge.

"That's it. That's the last book, the last chapter, the last sentence of the last paragraph, and not one single, solitary word about us."

Saedi sat down next to her friend and took his blue hand in her green one. "Maybe there are other libraries we can search—"

"No, Saedi." Gesturing with his free hand the vastness of the books freely embedded into the walls. "This is the last library. And this,"—he patted the book with his flat, fat hand—"was the last book. We've looked everywhere." He placed his hand over the two they held, and looked into her round, white eyes. "We're doomed to oblivion, I'm afraid."

"No. No, we can't be. Maybe someone is writing about us right this moment. Maybe..." Saedi kicked at a pencil. It rolled to the edge of a notebook, paused, and rolled back toward them a bit before coming to a stop.

"No more maybes. People aren't writing about us anymore. They're writing about celebrities, or about cooking, or...oh, I don't know...the same old thing a whole different way, I suppose. There are no new ideas, no new imaginings, just books and books about reality and things which already exist." Enigami stood, walked to the edge of the table, and looked down at the smooth wooden seat of its chair. "Doomed, we are."

"Come away from the edge, Eni. You're scaring me."

"You ought to be scared!" Enigami walked back over to his glossy friend. "Once we're gone, we're gone. G-O-N-E! No one jotted us down in the middle of the night to remind them at daylight of their spark of inspiration. We likely won't come back... together, anyway. I may show up alongside some dull idea. You could appear inside a blah imagination."

Eni bent down on one knee and took Saedi's hand. "Together, we're brilliant. Don't you see? We're perfect together. As we are. Today. In this moment."

"How can you be so sure we won't come back together? Someone else could pull us out together. It happened this time, it could happen again." Saedi looked into Eni's eyes. "It could."

"No. No, it won't. The time is perfect for us to exist now," Eni said. "This may be hard for you to hear, but you're not my first match. I've been down this road before, and through apathy, we were lost to oblivion. Saedi... you and I had only one chance to make this right, and I'm afraid we failed."

"Wait. What are you saying? There was one before me? You were with another before me?" Saedi stood with her back to Eni and held back a sob. "Were there more than the one? Or am I just another in a long line? Did you tell them the same lies you're telling me now? That we're perfect together? You're just saying that to save yourself." Saedi ran to the edge of the table and prepared to jump.

"Saedi! No—"

And that's when they saw me standing in the doorway, watching them. They appeared to be walking, talking *Gumby* dolls with spiky hair and bendable limbs. Walking. Talking. Sitting. Standing on a table in the middle of the closed library.

Just... unreal.

Saedi ran back and into the arms of Enigami. "I think he can see us. How can he see us, Eni?"

"I don't know. We may belong to him." Eni's eyes became small. "Stay close." He held Saedi tightly.

I took a step toward them. They took a step back. I took another step, then another. They matched me in reverse. They backed up to the edge of the book's spine and sat once more upon the book. They trembled in each other's arms.

"You're not supposed to be able to see us," Eni said.

"Then it would seem I'm doing the impossible," I said, leaning in to examine them. I put my face within slapping distance. Saedi obliged.

Her hand smacked the tip of my nose. It sounded like rubber hitting linoleum. I barely felt it, but flinched just the same. Eni smiled.

"Who...what are you guys?" I asked, pulling back and rubbing the tip of my nose.

"Nothing. At least, soon we'll be nothing," Eni said. He pulled Saedi even closer.

"I...I'm not understanding you," I said, sitting in the chair. "You look like something to me. Two distinct somethings." I reached out and gently touched one of the stubbly, blunt spikes on Saedi's head.

"Hey! Stop that!" She ducked her head and pushed at my finger.

"So cool..." Her hair felt like rubber.

Eni cleared his throat. "Pay attention, human. Only rarely is a magnificent idea born alongside a great imagination, and once melded together on paper, they birth a beautiful creation that will live on for eternity." Eni hugged Saedi. "We are that one perfect idea and imagination. Soon we'll disappear into the thin air from whence we came, never to be seen again. Together, anyway. Our brilliant spark will cease to exist or even be remembered for that matter, except for a slight pull you might feel in the recesses of your brain about a brilliant thought you once had but failed to act upon. You'll never again be able to conjure us.

"So you see, not only did you create us, but by failing to nurture us you'll eventually kill us."

"How is your plight my fault?" I asked.

"Don't you see? You've been given a gift of an idea." Saedi sat up a bit on the book and pointed one of her three fingers at me.

"And not just any idea, a brilliant one. You have a choice to write about us and make us live on, or forget about us and watch us fade away.

"Either way, your choice, your fault."

"What can I do?" I asked.

"Write about us. Write about us now before you forget. And then do something with the writings. Don't put us in a drawer. Sometimes that works out—one of your offspring or your landlord will open that drawer at some point after your death and find us—and then we may exist again." Eni's eyes brimmed with tears. "More often than not, though, we're forgotten. The house burns to the ground, or we're toted off in a cardboard box and into a storage shed or trash pile. Either way, our fate is the same. We disintegrate over time."

"Disintegrate. That's just a fancy word for die," Saedi said, placing her head on Eni's shoulder.

I picked up the pencil, and began writing in the notebook.

I kept writing.

The sun set and rose and set again. Eni and Saedi stood by, giving me suggestions and urging me on when I became stuck. I didn't stop writing until I'd finished the last sentence. Then together we revised and revised again, until the words were perfectly placed on the pages, not one word too many nor one too few.

I sat back in my chair, rubbed my growling stomach, and stretched my aching back.

Eni stopped pacing and read the last sentence aloud. "'THE LAND FELL AWAY FROM THE ROAD, LEADING TO A ROW OF ELM TREES, BEYOND WHICH LAY THE UNKNOWN.' That's... that's awesome," he said, patting me on the forearm. "Thank you, human. Because of you, Saedi and I will live forever."

Eni took Saedi's hand. "Are you ready?" he asked.

Saedi nodded.

I watched as they stepped onto the paper. Their bodies flowed into one and seeped into the written words, disappearing from the tangible and vanishing into the ethereal world.

I sped home and typed up the handwritten manuscript. I sent it off to a publisher I'd researched and believed to be the perfect house for it. I had pledged to Saedi and Enigami I'd not let them die. They would live forever in a book read and loved by millions.

Months later, I received a thick letter in the post. I held my breath as I carefully tore open the envelope.

This was it. We had our answer.

I sat down, pulled the typed response from its shell, and began to read:

"Thank you for submitting your manuscript for our review. Unfortunately, we find the text too didactic in feel for our tastes..."

Broken

Mollie's sun dress kicked up around her thighs as she sat looking out at her options. In front of her THE LAND FELL AWAY FROM THE ROAD, LEADING TO A ROW OF ELM TREES, BEYOND WHICH LAY THE UNKNOWN. To her right, her car grumbled and sighed in the barrow ditch, its grill crumpled around the stump of an oak. She touched the lump on her forehead and pulled away sticky crimson fingers. Wiping her fingers on the grass, she looked over to her left and the road leading back to him. Back to pain. Back to a certain death...of her soul, at least.

"Shit, Mollie. Don't be so fucking dreary." Her whispered voice echoed in the open space and drifted off in front of her. She imagined it floating through the elms. Then she stood and followed on unsure footing, in unsuitable shoes and without hesitation—leaving behind the wreckage of her life.

She'd taken no more than a hundred steps when her foot slipped into a hole, wrenching her ankle around.

"Ow! Shitshitshitshit. Shit!" *Now I ache at both ends,* she thought. *Thank you very much.*

She looked back at her car. Then she remembered her purse sitting on the front seat... oh, and her coat in the back... and the package of sunflower seeds open on the dash. Well, they were on the dash, before that damned rabbit darted out and scared the shit out of her and off the road.

Stupid, fucking bunnies. The road to hell is paved with stupid, fucking bunnies. This hole was probably dug by a stupid, fucking bunny. Stupid. Fucking. Bunnies. She bent over and clawed at the hole, attempting to release her trapped foot when a new pain shot up her leg.

She heard his car before she saw it, engine revving around the last bend so ostentatiously. She heard the tires squeal and then turned to see the bumper of his red Dodge Charger as it came into view, sidling up next to her wrecked Mustang. His window eased down. Mollie heard the rhythm of his radio, but couldn't make out the song. It pounded with the beat of her heart, hard and fast.

How in the hell did he find me?

"Come on, Mollie. Don't keep me waiting...again."

She couldn't see his face, just the point of his elbow resting on the car's window frame.

"Mah-lee..." in a sing-song voice.

She eased her foot out of the hole and tried to stand on it, gingerly at first but then applying her entire weight. Not too painful. A bit of a twinge, but...

"Mah-lee, you're starting to piss me ah-ahf..." Again with the sing-song, half-lilting, full-scary voice.

She looked back toward the elm trees. *I could make it. Could be halfway into the trees before he opens his door. I could—*

His horn tore her thoughts apart.

"Mollie! Get your fat arse in the car. Now!"

The hour-long drive back to his house was tedious, to say the least. She'd had time to grab her purse out of the wreck-age, but not her coat. She imagined she'd get an earful about wrecking the car, but he just listened to his radio rock on.

The air conditioner blasted, causing her bare arms and legs to riddle with goose bumps. Her nipples hardened against the thin cotton of her dress. She noticed him noticing her and grew hopeful when his hand reached for the air conditioner control. When he turned the temperature down, she looked out the window and tried not to cry.

Figures. Tits trump goose bumps. Men! She crossed her arms over her chest.

"You look a mess, Moll." He dug in his pocket, pulled out a handkerchief, and tossed it onto her lap. "At least clean the blood off your forehead. You're not nearly pretty enough to sport an open wound."

Mollie picked it up and searched for a soft, unused spot. She tried to ignore the gross, off-color lumps. She glanced over at him. His hands rested on the steering wheel at nine and three. His eyes darted between his rearview and sideview mirrors, never focusing on anything in particular. He sat rigidly straight, buckled and proper, as he'd done for the seventeen years she'd known him.

She spat on the edge of the cloth, pulled down the visor mirror, and examined her forehead. A bruise adorned the bloody cut. She dabbed at the wound, cleaning it as best she could.

"What were you doing so far out?" He smiled at her. His cold eyes looked right through her. A shiver ran down her spine. "You know better than to make me worry."

"Just...sorry...um..." *You have no idea how far away from you I wish to be.*

"Jestsorryum... You sound like an idiot. You know that, right?" He barked a laugh and then looked down at her nipples, pressed hard against the front of her dress. He adjusted himself. "Are you cold, babe?" He asked in a softer voice, raising his hand from his crotch to stroke her shoulder. It brought a chill with its warmth. Mollie tried to not pull away, but he must have felt her cringe. His grip tightened; his face pinched in anger.

"You know better than to be afraid of me." His voice almost made her pee.

"I know. I felt a little static shock when we touched, is all." Mollie looked out her window. *OurFatherwhoartinHeaven hallowedbeThynameThykingdomcome Thywillbedone...* She clamped her teeth and stifled a sound as she felt his hand migrate to her chest and linger over her nipple.

...onEarthasitisinHeavengiveusthisdayourdailybread...

His touches, even the more gentle ones made her skin crawl these days.

His breathing became wet and heavy, easily heard over his music.

"Let me just... adjust... your..."—his hand moved from her breast—"vents. There." He settled back into his seat. His hand rested on his distending crotch. "That's better, isn't it?"

"Yes."

"Yes, what?" He smiled.

"Yes, sir." She forced a smile.

They rounded a corner, and his house came into view. The air grew stale. He turned off the radio as he pulled into the driveway. The ring of keys clanked against the steering column, drawing her attention. She watched them sway back and forth, mesmerized by the glimmer as they caught the sunlight. The white rabbit foot did little to mute the clinking.

Stupid, fucking bunnies.

She feigned a headache and went straight to bed.

He came to her after sunset. She heard her door creak open in the dark. She listened to his footsteps grow closer. She felt the bed dip on what she thought of as "his" side of the bed, as he settled his bulky frame. She clutched her pillow. His meaty body pressed against her back; his hardness nestled between her cheeks, separated from him only by the thin nightgown she wore.

"Hey, babe. You feeling any better?" He rubbed himself against her. "You have some hefty apologizing to do. Cars don't come cheap. It's gonna cost a pretty penny to tow that baby tomorrow, too."

"I need to go potty." She pulled away from him and sat up. A wet spot on her nightgown stuck to the small of her back. "Did you take your medicine today?"

"Shit. No. I forgot. Grab it for me."

The water tasted refreshing. She took a deep breath and glanced around the bathroom. Bunny wallpaper. Bunny curtains. Even the glass she held was bunny-fied.

Stupid, fucking bunnies. I was that close to freedom.

She opened the medicine cabinet. Neat and orderly, exactly the way he liked it. She took out his medicine, and noticed the pearl-handled razor. He'd said it belonged to his grandfather.

Mollie placed the bottle on the counter and opened the razor. The blade glistened, sharper than any she'd seen. She pressed it against her wrist.

Remember, Mollie, one must cut upward to do the most damage.

"Mollie? You fall in?" His voice made her startle. She nicked her skin, and a bead of blood welled. She kissed it away.

"Coming..." She closed the blade and tucked it under her arm, grabbing his pills and the water.

The medicine bottle and empty glass sat on the bedside table. With heart pills dissolving in his stomach, he pulled her on top of him.

He pushed aside her underwear.

"Love you, babe," he said as he entered her. "You like this? Does this feel good?"

Must one always cut upward?

"Does this?" she asked.

The blade sliced neatly through his skin, windpipe, and arteries with little effort, which surprised her. Surprised him, too, judging by the look on his face. She stood, and watched as dark liquid flowed from his neck and soaked into the bed. It didn't spurt or spray, as she'd imagined. *Probably because of his fat.*

"Love you, too... Dad."

Blood dripped from the razor. SHE HELD IT IN ONE HAND AND REFLECTED ON THE SHOCKING SPEED AT WHICH HER FOR-TUNES HAD TURNED AROUND, A LONGED-FOR MOMENT THAT, EVEN AS IT REGISTERED ON HER, CEASED TO BE A GOAL AND BECAME A MEMORY.

"Mind if I take your car? Mine's broken."

Awkward

Jo's at the age where she's two different people: one on the inside, the other on the out.

If you're a mother of a daughter, or even a woman without, you know of what I speak.

I see the little girl in her. I notice the woman trying to emerge. It's both heartbreaking and amazing at the same time.

The other day she was taking a bath and she yelled at me to "Mawwwm, come here."

So I did.

She sat in a tub full of bubbles to her eyebrows and looked very much like a young woman. She handed me some tin cooking toys her dad had given Jack and her a bit ago. (Cooking toys = pots, pans, utensils, etc., all made out of flimsy tin... from China, no doubt.) The girls played with the toys in the bath in the past and they (the toys, not the girls) had rusted in the cupboard since.

"Take these away and toss them, please," she said. "They're gross. And there's more in here (indicated cupboard), but one has a spider web on it and I don't want to touch it."

I picked up the rusted toys and took them to the kitchen to toss. I came back for more. As I gathered up the plastic coffee maker with carafe, she reached out her hand and softly (and a tad embarrassed) said, "No, not that one. I'm playing with that."

My little girl who still plays with children's toys in the bath may look like she's ready for womanhood, but every real mother knows no matter how many clueless guys say she's hot or that they'd like to teach her a thing or two about being a "real" woman, she's still just a caterpillar trying to emerge from her chrysalis into the butterfly she will some-day become.

But not too soon.

Because, as you know, if a butterfly is forced or helped she'll never truly learn to fly.

Life isn't about sex. Nor is it about hotness.

I can't wait for the day we evolve (if we ever do evolve) into thinking, caring, loving beings who have more on our minds than sex with underage or hot young girls.

sigh

The Best You Ever Had

The best you ever had. Ha!

You were talking about sex.

What you didn't know is

She *was* the best

And I'm not talking about sex

And you threw her away

When you threw yourself into another her

And whoever else had a wet spot pointed at you

Yes, she is the best.

The best you ever *had*.

PS. Every girl has a wet spot...

Good luck with that

Parts Is Parts

My sister had what she considered a strange experience today. I don't think it was all that strange.

While she watched television, a commercial displayed a beautiful girl with puffy lips. The young, barely dressed female provocatively pranced in stiletto heels across my sister's television screen, enticing males of all ages to make a private visit to the bathroom of their choice to take matters into their own hands. I doubt if anyone knew what product she was selling.

My sister toughed it out until the end of the commercial, but after another commercial, the station played the offending commercial once more.

Strangely, she felt accosted by this dehumanization of the female body, so much, in fact, she almost lost her lunch. Thank God she hadn't eaten yet.

She expressed her feelings to me in a phone call.

I told her I feel the same way when the media uses the beautiful female physique to sell merchandise. I don't know why women—or fathers and husbands for that matter—allow themselves and other people to exploit women's beauty for nothing more than "sex sells" and a woody.

I wonder how a man would feel if it were his daughter parading in front of the camera for his sexual pleasure. "Surprise, Daddy. Are you proud of me now?"

I feel the same way when females think the only things they have to offer society are two firm nipple mounds and a camel toe.

As you might remember, I have five daughters. It disturbs me to know they are targeted by the media to feel less than adequate if they don't measure up to media's (men's?) idea of a sexual beauty.

It disgusted me when I found a DVD chock-full of scantily (if at all) clad, barely adult (if not teenagers) in my not-yet-ex-husband's possession. (It still does.) His excuse—they're just parts.

Just parts.

Just parts? Is that what we've allowed our female bodies to become to these socially acceptable perverts?

Just parts? When our young women are demonstrating wild girl-on-girl action and drunken show of frontal nudity to a camera so some guys can get... excited and others get rich from these barely un-children's impulsive actions.

Just parts? When your forty(plus)-year-old partner turns his head and walks into a nearby pole because he can't get enough of the twelve-year-old (who looks not a day younger than sixteen)'s breasts and tight pants? ...And seriously thinks that same girl wears a bikini to the beach or swimming pool for his pleasure—instead of for the boy she has a crush on who sits next to her in school.

Just parts? When you go to a movie, you know the director knows his vision sucks when he brings out the nipple parts. If you get a glimpse of the crotch parts, he knew his movie was in serious trouble. But when the long, drawn-out, don't-catch-me-yawning shot of the woman's OOOOhhh face, and shows nothing but the stud's back but all of the female parts—you know the director knows you'll never see this movie up for any kind of award. But you might see it in your son's or partner's sweaty hands at the video store. And that's all that matters, right?

Sex sells.

Females whore their parts out for profit. They sell their

souls to pay the rent; a decision they'll treasure for the rest of their lives, no doubt.

Just parts.

And when our parts are used up and tired out—which is the ultimate result in every case—are any of us surprised?

When we find the thirty-something, ex-beauty queen in the morgue too soon or out at the pub too late because her gravity-altered parts no longer please an audience, will we act surprised?

Since when is sex synonymous with a naked female, lips red with make-up and ready to go down on her knees at the first command?

Some might say I'm a frigid woman who's jealous because her own parts sag to her knees and she couldn't find her G spot with an alphabet ruler. Others might call me uptight and question if I simply find the female body disgusting.

I am not jealous my parts sag to my knees. It gives me something to put in my lap as I sit to ease the pain in my back.

My G spot is somewhere between my F and H spots.

I don't find the female body disgusting.

But I do find the exploitation of, and salivation over the female parts to be disturbing, to say the least.

If our parts are so natural and common, why use them provocatively to sell? What's all the hullabaloo about?

They are, after all, just parts.

Everything has parts—even my hair.

Does that turn you on?

We

We talked

We chatted

We laughed

We smiled

We shared

We dreamed

We cuddled

We caressed

We tasted

We touched

We loved

I thought I was enough for you

Until you found another

To talk with

To chat with

To laugh with

To smile with

To share with

To dream with

To cuddle with

To caress

To taste

To touch

To love

Is this new one enough for you?

I don't much care

But she might...

Because you'll soon find another

To talk with

To chat with...

You can't help it

It's in your nature

And she'll be enough

Until you find another.

Take It Back

You can have your necklace back.

It took me a while to realize you were just
stringing me along with a golden chain.

Hairy Experiment

I'm almost too embarrassed to tell you this.

You know how you get those helpful hint emails every now and again? The ones which tell you, for instance, vinegar can be used in more places than the bathtub?

Well, I got one. It swore Elmer's glue could be used as a facial mask to peel off dead skin and clear out blackheads.

I said to myself, "Oh. Homemade pore strips. Cool."

Um... not so much.

I washed my face with near scalding water to open my pores, smeared Elmer's glue from my widow's peak to my chinny-chin-chin and from ear lobe to ear lobe (and all places in between), and then waited, tight-lipped, for the glue to dry.

And when it did, I carefully lifted the edge and pulled—

Oh! My! God!

Do you remember (you may not be old enough) the spring-coil hair removal system which pulled the hair on your legs out by the root? It was touted as being ninety-eight percent painless... And here's news flash: the other two percent was what made you involuntarily pee your pants from the pain.

Okay, it was a lot like that.

I forgot tiny, angel-feather-like hair covers my face. Or did, rather, up until that point anyway.

After I stopped crying, blackheads didn't seem like such a problem anymore.

That Thing You Do

You said

She said

You were a great husband except for
the whole infidelity thing.

I now know what she meant by that.

Shoulda

You know what my problem is?

My problem is

I shoulda just used you

Like you were using me.

I shoulda not looked inside your eyes

While you were using me.

I shoulda not believed what you said

As you were using me.

I shoulda just used you back.

And after we were all used up

I shoulda just pushed you out the door

...Like you did me.

Beholder's Eyes

I was about eighteen and making pizzas at the local pizza joint alongside my best friend, Pete. He recalled the events of his past evening for my sole benefit while spreading cheese over sauced dough. Seems they'd gone to a bar where the entertainment (and I use the term lightly) was a wet t-shirt contest. His accolades for the winner wouldn't cease, so finally I said, "Yeah, well, I got boobs, too."

His reply was, "But she had a face and the bod to go with them."

Fast forward a bit to age twenty-one. My soon-to-be first husband and his cronies came over to my apartment to watch the Superbowl. As I passed around the brews and chips, the guys swapped stories about this fox and that chick. Animals, it seems, are all women are to them.

In the middle of the laughter and stories, my guy looked at me and said to the manly crowd in a loud and determined voice, "Sandi's not much to look at, but she's got one hell of a personality."

Not for the first time, nor the last, I wished I'd perfected the vanishing skills I practiced so often as a child.

Fast forward to many years later and soon-to-be second ex-husband. We were attending a hail-and-farewell (Army thing) and husband couldn't stop flirting, touching, and ogling one stunning captain—one of many young ladies in his long line of ego-girlfriends. His wildly inappropriate actions were beginning to embarrass me, but I kept quiet until the ride home. I asked him if he thought the young woman he doted on was pretty.

(I know, you shouldn't ask the question if you don't want to hear the answer.)

"Yes," he said, "very pretty."

"Do you think I'm pretty?"

"Well, you're not ugly. I wouldn't be with anyone who wasn't at least a little pretty."

Hit that fast forward button to a few months ago. I was at a conference minding my own business, grabbing a cup of coffee at break-time, when a portly, much older gentleman approached me and said, "You know, I have to tell you. I find you to be a very striking woman."

"Why, thank you. That's sweet." Dumbstruck, my ego-balloon started to inflate a bit. Those were words I was unaccustomed to hearing.

"Yes, very striking. I don't know when I've seen such a striking woman before."

(I became a little uncomfortable at that point, but that damned balloon hung on every word and grew bigger than my head.)

"Thank you," I said again, and smiled politely.

He continued to look at me with what was increasingly becoming more of a leer, and added, "Not beautiful by any means... but striking."

POP!

There went that balloon.

I wonder if anyone else heard it.

Symmetry

She gave her first hand job when she was just 15.

She gave her last one at 51.

There's poetry in that.

Prepositional Lover

I thought you were into me...

And then she got under you...

And now I have to get over you...

Like you got over me...

When she came under you.

Spackled

She was just another hole for you to fill.

You've filled it, thank you.

Mark her off your life

And move along.

Sexy, Sexy, Sexy!

I sent the kids to school. The television was on...crowd noise, you know. *E! THS Investigates: Serial Killers* came on. I heard an announcer say "two to four percent of the population are psychopaths... so, they're out there."

Which made sense.

Statistics show you're more likely to be a psychopath than you are to be allergic to anything, even peanuts. Maybe you're both.

Hiding in plain sight.

Yesterday the girls were home sick—not to be confused with homesick. Anyway, I zoned out between running hot tea to one, soup to the other. On one channel (I can't remember) the fifty cutest childhood stars (and where are they now)—a program from 2005.

I wasn't really watching, rather semi-observing.

Did you know if a boy childhood star makes it through *Growing Pains*—surviving fame at such an early age to become someone as productive as, say, Opie Cunningham, the media labels them as intelligent trend-setters of fantastical degree? Whereas if a girl childhood star makes it through puberty, tracking the same path as her childhood male co-star, she's no more than sexy, sexy, sexy! regardless of what she's done in the days since. Unless you're someone like Natalie (Mindy Cohn) from *Facts of Life*, that is—then you're funny. (I was unaware she'd been working pretty much solidly from about 1980 on. Amazing, really..)

My sister conveyed a story to me yesterday she thought was funny. Normally she dresses rather well before leaving the home, whether she's going to work, or just out and about. Her husband rarely comments on her attire one way or another. He's not being rude, mind you. It seems he doesn't take notice—or maybe just doesn't comment.

At any rate, as she prepared to go to work on a project with a friend, she donned some old and ratty, stained overalls.

Her husband walked in the room and asked, "What are you getting all dolled up for?"

...Sexy, Sexy, Sexy!

You Said

You said she's special.

You said you adore her.

You said she's the best you ever had.

You said.

You said you love her.

You said you really like her.

You said you like her.

You said she's sweet.

You said...

She heard what you said.

You said you'd call.

You said you'd visit.

You said you are hers.

You said she is yours.

You said so many things.

She believed what you said.

But your actions spoke louder

Than your saids.

You held another.

You touched another.

You kissed another.

You tasted another.

You made another giggle.

You made another moan.

You made another yours.

You put another in her place;

You put her in her place.

You said

You liked her.

She no longer believes in your saids.

No Strength Left

I don't have the strength it takes to go through another you.

You said you were safe.

You weren't.

It Is What It Is

Love is Trusting

Sharing

Hearing

Caring

Knowing

Learning

Growing.

Love isn't Lying

Cheating

Hurting

Leaving

Taking

Sneaking

Faking.

You're right...

You don't know love

Relationships 101: Domination

ATTENTION!

Guys and Gals,

If you're confused as to what subservience is, if you've often wondered to yourself how you can show the object of your desire the depths of your superiority, this is the class for you! With our expert guidance, you'll find yourself on the way to moving from being a simple significant other (S.O.) to becoming a world-class unequivocal S.O.B.

In this class, we'll teach the fundamentals of partner self-esteem dismantling and complete S.O. control.

If your S.O. has gotten out of line by not reporting in at a time you deem to be the deadline, we'll teach you the skills of debasement and harassment. You'll have your S.O. groveling at your feet in no time.

If the disobedience keeps up, we teach you valuable skills in Forceful Verbal Negotiations (FVN). You'll learn such phrases as: Don't bother, where the fuck were you, and don't write about me ever again.

When FVNs no longer work and your non-compliant excuse of an S.O. fails to respond to other demeaning verbal commands, we offer one-on-one instruction on email etiquette.

You'll learn to eloquently write such treasures as:

hey it was poker night should have been here had a blast..... every one got a kick out of your e mail seeings how 99 % of it was bull shit, and

Do not take this rebutal as a reason for you to come back

to me, you are not welcome in my life any more."

Yes. We'll even unteach you how to spell.

But wait! There's more.

If you act now, we'll teach you the lost art of phone fantasy, where you can call your S.O. up to ten times a day, alternating between begging and insults.

We also teach you the Ploy Skill of calling and acting concerned for your S.O.'s safety. That's sure to get an immediate reaction.

We guarantee results in no time.

But if by chance our teachings fall short and your S.O. fails to respond in an adequate and contrite manner, we offer the following class at no additional cost (limited time offer). Yes, that's right, folks. We will enroll you in our follow-up class at no cost to you whatsoever.

Act now! Become the best S.O.B. you can be!

Relationships 102: Revenge

Follow our step-by-step instructions here:

1. Turn off your S.O.'s cell phone service, but don't stop there. Change the number so your S.O. is unaware anything is up. No one will be able to contact your S.O. and you will be in complete control of all incoming calls.

2. Throw all of your S.O.'s belongings in trash bags and set them outside in the elements, preferably in the middle of the night during a thunderstorm or blizzard. Money saving hint: skip the trash bags.

3. Show up at S.O.'s door early in the morning, perhaps six or six thirty. Demand your stuff back. When asked if you brought the S.O.'s things, say in the most vile voice you can muster, "You can pick it up yourself." Follow your acrid retort with a single question to disarm the S.O. "So... is there any hope we can get back together?"

4. Retrieve the cell phone and debit card for the joint checking account from your S.O. Don't forget to pick up your passport and extra keys. (Leave all gates open and make as much of a mess as possible—it adds points to your final test grade.) Remember, you left these things with your S.O. for safe-keeping, so you wouldn't have to be responsible for such valuable items, but make it appear as if your S.O. "stold" them from you.

5. Start writing harassing and nasty one-liner responses on your S.O.'s blog or website. Misspell every other word and use absolutely no punctuation. It gets the point across

much better. Don't bother sticking with reality; just make up stuff as you go along. Accuse your S.O. of having one or more sexual encounters with other people. (Ensure you spread this throughout your group of friends and neighbors for continuity. This strategy will make the lies seem more truthful. Remember, no proof is necessary. Accusations are acceptable.) Use your S.O.'s most vulnerable secrets. For instance, maybe your S.O. is insecure as to how good of a parent she or he is, and confided that to you. This is the exact time to divulge those secrets to the masses.

6. Call your S.O.'s neighbors and randomly question the whereabouts of your S.O.'s vehicle. You may alternate this action with driving by on a regular basis. Disregard the fact you've been to your S.O.'s house more times this week than you have during your entire three-year relationship.

7. Cancel your S.O.'s offspring's plane tickets. You'll have to be tricky with this one, as you'll have to be willing to break at least one federal law. You'll also have to find an airhead miscreant to pose as your S.O. to cancel said tickets. Pick someone obtuse or brain-dead to do this, as they are breaking a federal law. Therefore, ensure you care not an iota for the nimrod you recruit.

8. Send your S.O. an extortion email claiming to have "6 pics of you you might not want any one to see" and end the email with a request for money you claim as "stold"

9. Sabotage your S.O.'s back tires by punching a roofing nail through the sidewall of one and a wood screw through the other, knowing full-well your S.O. and offspring are likely to be driving up to Denver in the wee morning hours to catch that flight you tried to cancel. If all works out well, a double blow-out will teach your S.O. some mighty valuable lessons in noncompliance and the consequences of actions.

10. Steal flowers meant for your S.O. from your S.O.'s front doorstep while your S.O. is away. This is especially fruitful as you (if you paid attention to Relationship 101

classes) rarely purchased flowers for your S.O. Give them to the cranial-vacant poser from #7 or toss them into the trash. It doesn't matter if they were from a family member who only wanted to brighten your S.O.'s day. Remember, your S.O. doesn't deserve anything nice. After all, your S.O. disobeyed you.

11. Keep the domination motto at the front of your mind always: If you love something, set it free. If it comes back to you, it's yours. If it doesn't—hunt it down and kill it.

I Hope

You'll never know the happiness you passed on,

But I hope you do

Someday.

And I hope your heart breaks then

Like hers is breaking now,

Today.

I hope she stops hurting soon.

I hope she starts healing soon.

I hope she can learn to trust again, but not too soon.

I hope when someone else says he adores her

...Or finds her beautiful

Or says she's the best thing that ever happened to him,

I hope he's telling her truth.

I hope she hears his voice in her head,

And not yours.

I hope she can believe him

Like she believed you.

And I hope he means it,

Like you didn't.

And I hope he loves her

Like you couldn't.

And I hope he never does to her

What you did to her.

I hope.

PS. Where did you put her heart?

She might need it again someday.

No hurry.

Come Again Soon

Happy?

What do you know about happy?

You know how to win a heart.

You know how to take.

You know how to drink nectar from my soul.

You know what to say.

When to say it.

How to say it.

How to lie,

And lie.

I'm waiting.

Soon.

Soon, you said

You'd be here soon.

You said you'd be here soon;

You promised you'd be coming soon.

I'm still waiting.

You said you'd come.

I thought you meant here,

Come here to be with me.

I didn't know you meant

Coming soon

Inside another.

I can't believe I fell for your lies.

How stupid am I?

Come again soon,

But don't show up at my door.

Happy at the End of My Rope

I recently got sucked into Facebook by an old friend. ...That's how they get you.

So, anyway, I started poking around and found some other old friends—um, not 'old' necessarily. How about friends from my past?—on Facebook as well. Strange how no matter how much time passes you still feel eighteen, and you still think about people from your past from time to time.

Much of my chapter book series: The Elementary Adventures of Jones, JEEP, Buck & Blue incorporated my friendships in my past—high school, junior high, elementary school neighbors, friends and foes—as well as from my present. I owe them all a debt of gratitude. I can honestly say there was no one I didn't care for in my home town as I grew up... 'cept maybe that one dude.

Don't get me wrong—there were some girls horrifically horrible to me growing up, especially in gym class. I was a late bloomer. A friend made fun of that fact and teased me unmercifully in the shower: "Maybe if you shave down there, the hair will grow back darker... Oh, my God, I think she's tried it!!! *AHAHAHahahahahaha*." Yeah, a real laugh-riot. And, no I didn't shave back then. (Don't ask me about now, unless you really want to know the answer!) And the ever-so-original: "Them ain't boobs, them are bee stings!" hahaha ...*funny*.

Two girls of the popular variety used to love to aim for my face in dodge ball. I think it was a personal goal of theirs to break my glasses, or my nose...maybe my spirit. I am unsure.

Yep, I pretty much hated gym class. It didn't help that as a freshman I was about as physical as a snail, weighed all of seventy-five pounds at four feet, eleven inches tall. *Go, Tigers!*

Seriously, though, can anybody climb that frickin' rope and touch the ceiling? And, what exactly is the purpose of possessing that specific talent?

I'm currently working on the next series: Stuck in the Middle with Jones, JEEP, Buck & Blue and was considering a series for when they're in high school as well. How does "Getting High with Jones, JEEP, Buck & Blue" sound? No? Well, send in your suggestions then, because I'm pretty much stuck.

How about: High Expectations of JJBB? Anyone? Anyone?

The phone lines will remain open until midnight tonight Vote early, vote often.

Perfect Fit

No such thing as a perfect fit.

They all fit.

They're one-size-fits-all.

They all grip you

Whether you're soft or hard

Or little or huge.

It fits.

It's supposed to.

I hope you know when you're not in it

Another one fits just as well,

Sometimes better.

And when another he is in her

She'll forget how well you fit.

She can fit anyone, too.

She can forget anyone, too.

I wonder sometimes if you miss her.

I know you don't.

You can't;

You're fitting another.

And you've forgotten

How perfect you said

You fit her.

I Thought

I thought you said...

I coulda swore...

You said 'adore.'

Maybe what you meant to say

Was 'abhor.'

How can you adore her, and treat her that way?

It makes more sense you abhor her.

Since it was so easy, for you

To treat her, for you

That way.

I Pray

Dear God,

He won't have your eyes.

He won't tell your lies.

He'll hold me tightly.

He won't treat me lightly.

He'll be gentle and true.

He'll be nothing like you.

Please, God.

Achieving Peace & Love...
and Total Enlightenment

Since it's July 7, first off I want to wish Ringo Starr and David a *Happy Birthday* today. I hope Ringo's birthday wish of "Peace & Love" comes true.

As for David...

I attended North Side Elementary School in my little town. While in second grade, Mrs. Polson marked all of our birthdays on her calendar, and when it came to my turn, I said in a weak, pathetic voice, "July second."

David, a classmate I didn't know (as this was the first day of school) jumped up and said, "Seventh? July seventh? Your birthday is the seventh? So's mine!"

At that point I wanted so much *not* to disappoint, but apologetically said, "No, the second."

David sat back down all dejected-like and said, "Oh..."

So *Happy Birthday, David*. I hope you're more satisfied with sharing Richard Starkey's birthday than mine.

I have two revelations to make on this day. As I drifted off to sleep last night, I realized God is more than likely a female. She gives us a clue in the way She dictated the Ten Commandments.

Let me explain. (I've copied the following verbatim from one of my many bibles.)

1. Thou shalt have no other Gods before me. Thou shall not make unto thee any graven image, or any likeness of

anything [cross? statues?] that is in heaven above, or that is in the earth beneath, or that is in the water underneath the earth. Thou shalt not bow down thyself to them, nor serve them, for I the LORD thy God am a jealous God. [Now isn't that exactly what a woman would say? Yeah, only a woman would put that much detail into her demands.]

2. Thou shalt not take the name of the LORD thy God in vain. [I personally believe that to mean you shalt not make money off the name of God...but that's just me. And I'm a woman.]

3. Remember the Sabbath [Saturday] and keep it holy. ['Modern' man changed it to Sunday.]

4. Honor thy father and thy mother. [Yeah, an all-powerful man would even remember to mention a mother in a day and age when females were little more than chattel.]

5. Thou shalt not kill. [My mom preached that message to us kids 24/7. And my dad always tried to kill us. I'm just saying...]

6. Thou shalt not commit adultery. [I think a man would have left that one out, period.]

7. Thou shalt not steal. [I believe either gender would agree with that one.]

8. Thou shalt not bear false witness against thy neighbor. ["I did not have sexual relations with that woman..."]

9. Thou shalt not covet thy neighbor's house, thou shalt not covet thy neighbor's wife, nor his manservant, not his maidservant, not his ox, nor his ass, nor anything that is thy neighbor's. [Okay—why would a man covet his neighbor's ass?]

I never really found a tenth commandment. It looks to me the religions split number one into two, but they're basically the same. Maybe 'Nine Commandments' wasn't as catchy or left the tablets lop-sided?

My second revelation for today is I think my mother is going loop-de-loop.

Her own revelation this weekend causes me to think such things. Somewhere in her vast search for "the truth" she came across an article about an eighty-year-old woman, who—in a controlled experiment, mind you—tripped on Magic Mushrooms and achieved total enlightenment. So now Mom feels she'd like to take that Magical Mystery Tour herself. (You're welcome, Ringo.)

Um, two things you really don't want to hear your mother say: "I've sold the house so you'll need to find another place to live," when you're barely sixteen, and "I'd like to start experimenting with crazy-arsed drugs," thirty-some years later. Especially when you're absolutely, positively against mind-altering drugs.

Period.

The Color of Poverty

I'm reminded how all people are so very much the same. My perceived owwies aren't the same as yours, but they're equal in hurt and personal emotional equity.

My eldest asks why I post certain things in my blog—like the embarrassment of my period painting my pants for all to see when I was seventeen or being chastised and threatened for opening my brain-works and heart to you. The simple answer is: It's cathartic... and hopefully it shows you are not alone.

We may handle life's little unpleasant gifts differently, but we are all relatively the same, I think.

For example, I believe we fall into one or more of these categories:

Some of us quietly work through personal struggles with smiles painted on our faces. We speak to peers and people in hushed, positive tones and do what we can to hide our fears and heartaches. No one knows we're slowly suffocating inside, trying to do and say the "right" thing and live the "right" way. We share our deepest thoughts only with our diary, if that. Our motto is: I have to and can do this alone and therefore worthy. We suffer in silence.

Some of us display our pain on our faces as a badge of honor. We openly share our perceived owwies as someone else's fault—and go everywhere and anywhere for a hand-out. We take every possible avenue from Entitlement Street, but still feel we're not getting our Fair Share when we perceive someone as having more than us. We claim to be one of TLF (the Less Fortunate) or PUS (Poor Unfortunate Souls). We deserve better, but we take what you will give us until we can get you to give us more. Our motto is: I am this way because this happened to me and therefore worthy. We suffer on display.

Some of us try to mask any pain we feel from our perceived owwies (or alleviate our guilt of having while others have not) by giving to the self-identifying (or those we deem as) PUS and TLF. We do our best to enable them, and we get our "good for you" rewards at the end of the day. We get to feel better about ourselves. We feel honestly justified to chide others who aren't as publicly giving and kind. Our motto is: I am giving, and therefore worthy. We suffer magnanimously.

There are more categories, but my point is we all suffer and strive to survive in our own little ways.

I want to say—regardless of the suffering or how we handle it—we're all worthy.

I write my innermost thoughts (albeit now slightly dampered as what I write will be used against me in the court of child custody, no doubt), because I want to share some of those thoughts and disjointed opinions with others who, like me, feel alien in this world. I am in this world, but not of it.

I believe I don't fall into any of the categories posted above. If I ever give to anyone, you'll never know about it because unlike the third category, I don't want—nor do I need—anyone to know how special I am; how giving I am. Nor do I wish to embarrass anyone I might help by publicly announcing my assistance to them. Unlike category two I'd rather not let anyone know how destitute I am, or have been, or might become. And unlike category one, I have far too big a mouth.

But that doesn't make any one of those categorically-labeled humans bad. It merely makes them human, a category in which I do fit—regardless of how many times I like to declare I'm from another planet.

I think most of us fit into the category: Why didn't I get the human rule book the first day of my comprehension like everyone else around me seems to have gotten... and read? Because I feel like I don't belong here. And I feel like everyone understands the rules when I don't. I feel like a fish in the headlights of this fast-moving vehicle called life.

The thing is, I think we all feel like that on some level. We mask it with our own badges of honor. One displays the BADGE OF EDUCATION and takes a seat. Another might cling to the BADGE OF SEXUAL ABUSE and takes a seat. Yet another snatches the BADGE OF WOE-IS-ME. Doesn't matter. We all get to claim a badge and take a seat. There're enough seats for everyone.

Recently, I received an email from my cousin. It was one of those "rules for life" memes which roam from inbox to inbox. One of the rules was something like: If everyone threw their problem in one big pile and saw everyone else's problems juxtaposed with their own, they'd snatch their own back in a heartbeat. I believe there's some truth in that.

Tuesday at work I was told I needed to take a class in poverty awareness.

The comment made me smile inside.

(I'm baring a bit more of my soul here for you than I really feel comfortable doing.)

I'm unsure if I was told that because of the color of my skin, or the absence thereof (color, not skin), or what. Because the conversation I was having had nothing to do with any-thing, so it hadn't been anything I said. It was thrown at me as a side thought.

Later, when I considered it a bit, I chose to become a little insulted. I'm sure the person had no idea when she said it how insulting it might be, as one might have, without knowing another, certain perceptions about that other person. I dress well-*ish*, and I try to speak intelligently. I try to carry myself in a certain manner. But my outward appearance ... let's just say you shouldn't judge a book by its cover.

I'd not have been so crass as to assume since her skin was darker than mine she'd been raised in poverty. That would've been perceived as racist on my part.

But when it comes to poverty...well, worn-out hand-me-downs from an older brother doesn't make a little girl feel very pretty.

I was raised with a burnt wooden spoon in my mouth... when I wasn't being beaten with it.

I thought "silver" was a color of another broken crayon.

And I will say (as I smile and shake my head), once upon a time, for more than a few years I went without food at times so my kids had enough to eat. We ate spaghetti every night because it was cheap. I washed clothes in the bathtub after the kids went to bed, and hung them all over the house to dry (the clothes, not the kids). The four of us lived in a small, two-bedroom apartment. The rooms were so small our dressers had to be crammed into the closets. The narrow hallway *was* the kitchen.

I haven't purchased any new clothes (or anything for that matter) for myself in over four years because my kids' needs come first.

You do what you got to do to survive.

Hell, I could teach a class on poverty awareness.

Now you understand my amusement at her words and the insult I felt later because she saw my pink skin and assumed my life had been all high heels and proper grammar —ergo, privileged.

I believe only one family in that little Wyoming town where I grew up faired worse than mine. I wouldn't know, mind you, but I believe it to be true. Because they took hand-me-downs from us, you see.

Poverty? Yes.

Poor Unfortunate Soul? No.

One of The Less Fortunate? By whose standards?

My skin is pink. Our pains and suffering are different, yet equal.

I owe you nothing.

You owe me the same.

Green Me

Hey! I recently came up with a fantastical idea.

You know how America is reportedly now the number one leading developed country in greenhouse gas emissions? At least that's what they said on NPR this morning...

Oh, watch out—here comes a tangent. Is America number one in greenhouse gas emissions or number one in developed countries? If it's the latter, that really isn't telling us much. What country, overall, emits the most greenhouse gases? And how do they know that?

Anyway, I was thinking—those of you who read my blogs know this can be a dangerous pastime. What if the greenies of America, like the celebrities and movie stars, find themselves trying to jump on the King of Green's bandwagon (that would be Ed Begley Jr.) and don't know quite how to go about it? I have a plan. *Mua ha ha ha ha.*

Celebrity A takes the money she would have spent on Poor Unfortunate Soul, Child B (from some country we've yet to pronounce correctly), who is in dire need of a laptop...and instead puts it into greening up a house in a neighborhood near you. They could even make a reality TV show about it. You know, solar panels, windmills, gardens, the whole nine yards (which I'm told is a real oogy military term relating to shooting off all the rounds of ammunition, but that's not the topic today, so get on with it), and in the process one more American home is conformed to saving the planet, one house at a time.

You may say, "Yes, but then American family C who recently had their house redone by Celebrity A will only sell said house with the benefit of having been worked on by said celebrity," to which I say, "Does it matter? The house is still 'green' and living off the grid. Better for all of us in the long run, right?"

This way all of these people with disposable incomes could really make a difference in the land they proclaim to love... well, at least love enough to find the loopholes in tax breaks.

Hey! Even better. We could figure out a way this "Green Me, Green My House" TV Show could be tax deductible to Daddy Greenbacks, instead of taking one percent of their income outside our borders to help children in foreign countries get laptops. This also helps out those of us who are truly wanting to get off the grid and become solar or wind efficient, but may never make enough money in our lifetime to succeed in that particular dream.

Which brings me to another question: If I make twenty-three thousand dollars a year, and give twenty percent of that to a charity, and Paris Hilton only gives one percent of her daddy's income, who is giving more and who is more giving?

On the surface, looking only at the amount of money given, it would seem Paris is both... But even if I gave it all, Paris would still be giving more just by donating one percent, yet I've given (hypothetically) all I have. And those who 'have' have only given one percent, which is close to nothing, comparatively. Just laptops (I mean food) for thought.

Anyway, back to "Green Me, Green My House." Movie stars and celebrities alike could really make a difference, and the show could be hosted by the King of Green himself. What do you say, Ed? Are you up for it?

(I want royalties for the idea. Don't worry, one percent of Angelina Jolie's annual income will be fine. Please make that tax-free. Thanks.)

Shades of Gray

My daughter, Jack, came up to me yesterday as I mopped the kitchen floor. Seems her classmates were doing a section on Abraham Lincoln and slavery in America and she needed an immediate answer to her questions.

Why is it tiny people seldom notice when moms clean? And why are all menial tasks typically allotted to the female of the species? It's because we have boobs, isn't it? They keep us balanced from the weight of the broom, mop, or dust rag, don't they?

...But I'm off topic.

"Mom, are we North or South?"

(Clueless, mopping Mom) "West."

"No, I mean: Are we on the side of the North or the South?"

I stopped mopping and looked at the paper she held.

"Oh. Um...neither, sweetie. Most of our ancestors were in Europe during that time. Except, of course, our great-great something-or-other Chief Red Eagle, who was in the West at the time."

She looked at me as if I had said we were living on Venus.

"But were we on the side of the North or South? Do we believe in slavery? Were we racists?"

"Uh...well, slavery is not a good thing, but it's not a racial thing. It's a human rights issue. Not all slave owners were white, and not all slaves were black."

She looked at me like a fish in the headlights, and—not for the first time—I wondered what the history books weren't teaching our children. Or how political correctness is rewriting history.

"Sweetie," I said, "People were brought over here from all over the world, from all walks of life. Some worked on the plantations, some on the railroad, the infrastructure... some made dental impressions in clay to bind them into servitude. They called them 'indentured slaves.' Once they came to North America, they found they were unable to work off their indebtedness, becoming slaves, like others who were sent here from their own counties, sold by their own people into slavery..."

I saw her blank eyes looking back at me.

"But were we on the side of the North or South?" she asked again.

And apparently that's what they're teaching our children—the "black" and "white" of it.

So like any good parent in this situation, I said, "West. Get over it."

Then I picked up my mop and continued mopping the grime from the floor, realizing the only real slaves left in America all have boobs and are named Mom by their owners.

If I Ran the World...

News would be news:

No special (human) interest emotional hostage material. That's why we have shows like *Entertainment Tonight*.

I would make it illegal to report anything about any movie star or celebrity unless they died or were in a horrible accident and their life was hanging on by a thread. And once they've died, report it and move on. How long has it been since we buried Anna Nicole? Other than that, I don't care what drugs or sexual/party activities in which Paris Hilton/ Lindsey Lohan/Britney Spears (fill in the blank-stare) is involved. And I really truly couldn't care less about their politics. Oh, and publishing houses wouldn't be allowed to publish any books written by celebrities or movie stars unless they knew how to put a complete sentence together in an informative or entertaining way without the help of a ghost writer. (Do I file Madonna's children's stories next to her sex book in my home library, or what? Oh, never mind. I didn't buy any books by Madonna.)

Sports tallies and information would be relegated to sports channels. Sports aren't news, they're games.

Weather would be reported on *The Weather Channel*. Weather isn't news. (Fire isn't weather. Blue skies are weather.)

And the newscasters would look less like models and more like the people you trust. There wouldn't be the ad-lib chit-chat. [Have you ever put the news on mute with closed captions? It actually says "ad-lib" when the talking heads are talking to each other's head between segments.] And I wouldn't be able to tell what their politics were by listening to their words and attitudes on what they report. Can we say "nonpartisan" and "unbiased"? Additionally, I think I would try to stop them from trying to be funny... the jury is out on this one, though. Sometimes they say something outrageous and it makes my day.

We wouldn't hear the heart-wrenching stories on the news of one family in a million who has "literally lost everything," as if no one else in any other state ever lost anything. We not only get to hear it, we get to hear it every fifteen minutes and on every flipping news channel.

If I ran the world, I would make credit cards illegal and expose them for what they truly are: legalized loan-sharking that's crumbling our economy. Or at least make it illegal to charge interest on interest on interest. Same goes for variable interest rate home loans.

If I ran the world, I would criminalize HMOs and health insurance. Enough of paying the middle guy to pay only a percentage of your medical bills, leaving you to pay the rest. That's a great return on your investment. Not!

If I ran the world, animals wouldn't be more important than children. And American children wouldn't be less important than children in third-world countries, even when it came to movie stars adopting one for publicity: animal or child. American children wouldn't be more important, just not less.

If I ran the world, perverts and pedophiles wouldn't be allowed to hide behind our first amendment rights. It's not just their first amendment right, you know. Non-citizens wouldn't hold more weight and have more rights in our United States courts and country than U.S. citizens.

If I ran the world, no one would be allowed to trample on someone else's rights. No one would be abused or mistreated because of someone else's actions or beliefs.

If I ran the world, there would be no drugs, no abuse, and no violent crimes.

Everyone would be happy.

...And then we all woke up!

Work With Me Here

I find it entertaining when someone is trying to persuade you into doing or thinking what they're thinking or doing, they say to you (in one form or another), "Work with me here."

Work with me here...

The school district bans peanuts and other nuts. I asked the reason behind their logic and I got, "Work with me here," from the school, from rabid bloggers, and from other opinionated parents. So... no nuts allowed.

That's it? That's the compromise? No. That's the world bending to your wishes.

Compromise: A settlement of differences in which each side makes concessions.

What concession, exactly, does the school district and the peanut-blogger mom make when they ban peanuts?

Someone with whom I used to be involved would say, "Work with me here" when I didn't agree with his decision.

And why should I agree every time? We are two separate individuals with two separate likes and dislikes. Just because we were a couple didn't mean our brains melded. It's my life, too.

Never, not once, did the man concede.

"Work with me here" really seems to mean, "Do it my way or else..." No working it out involved.

The religious sects, whether Christian, Jewish, Muslim, Buddhist, or Wiccan—I don't have enough time to list them all—all want the other one to "work with me here" by allowing prayer in school, but no chanting in the streets... light the Empire State Building in green, but don't you dare put up a Christmas tree in public... None of your religious decorations allowed, but here, hang this one up to represent mine.

I think my favorite religious irony is (once upon a time, anyway) when a service member and his or her family were stationed in Saudi Arabia, they were instructed to leave their Bibles, Hanukkah or Christmas decorations, and any other religious paraphernalia at home or it all would be confiscated and/or destroyed. That included the rosary beads your great-grandmother gave you—even if you didn't practice Catholicism, and they were now more of an heirloom. If you were in Saudi Arabia for two to four years or more, the family Bible stayed in storage in America. The service member doing a tour for the United States had to follow the rules and customs of the host country. Period. No negotiations. No compromise. Just work with me here.

Now, someone from the Mideast [which I still think should be what we call Ohio, Illinois, Indiana, etc., because on a US map it looks to me like the Midwest is Montana, Wyoming, Colorado] comes to America, we bend over backwards not to insult their religious beliefs, and we actually debate in court the practice of taking their pictures with their burqas on for drivers' licenses.

And on that—taking Muslim women's pictures with their faces covered because it's against their culture/religion to show their faces in public. Isn't it against their culture and religion to drive? Am I the only one who sees the irony in this? Or maybe I'm misinformed.

Work with me here...

When I lived in Georgia and the good Southerners learned I wasn't from the South, the first statement from their mouths was, "You must be a Yankee!" And when I lived in New York, the people there assumed I *must be* from the South.

People, work with me here! There's a whole bunch of

American real estate west of the Mississippi River. It's got Wal-Marts and everything.

More and more congressmen and women ask us to work with them to come to a compromise on health care, illegal immigration, and their annual pay raise. But what they're really saying is, "Get ready to bend over."

The Price of Convenience

I ordered a pizza last night. I asked for it to be delivered, one of the few perks in life and the only place which delivers any kind of (dare I call it food?) edible sustenance in my little town. The young man (by the sound of his voice) who called himself Joe asked if I would be paying with cash, check, or charge.

I told him I'd have to see what the damages were before I made that decision, but probably cash...

He read back my order and gave me a grand total of...

I told him I'd have to pay with check as I had just enough and not any for tip.

"Wait a minute, then. If you pay with check it's twenty-five cents more."

"What? Why?"

"Because that's what our manager makes us charge for checks..."

Twenty-five cents? Really? That's like... too little to matter, and not enough to make sense. More of an annoyance than anything else. "Tell your manager I think he's ridiculous."

"I don't think I should do that." I think that's what he said anyway. He was laughing.

"Oh... no, maybe you shouldn't."

Did you know they add an additional delivery fee and tip to your total, too?

Nope, me neither....

When the girl delivered the pizza to my door, I told her I was extremely sorry, but I would have to charge her manager a porch fee of one dollar. A strange expression crossed her face, not sure if I joking, and asked me why.

I said, "Oh, I'm sorry. I thought we were all now practicing levying arbitrary fees for obscure reasons."

We went to the local carnival and I ordered one small drink for two dollars—for the girlies.

The pimply-faced girl behind the counter informed me they didn't have small drinks.

I inquired as to why they had *small* indicated on their menu board.

She repeated they didn't have any small drinks, as they were currently out of small cups.

I looked at the price of a medium, which was three dollars, and said, "How convenient," and ordered a medium.

She handed me a huge, Styrofoam cup ...with no lid. (Hasn't anyone told these people about Styrofoam and our environment?)

"Can I get a lid?"

"Nope."

For three dollars, you'd think they could afford to give me a lid.

"Um, why not?"

"We don't have any."

"Oh, how ...inconvenient."

"We only have lids for the small cups," she said.

...And you wonder why I'm glad I'm not from this planet.

PC Playground

The more I listen to people around me, the more I hear their dissatisfaction over the tired idea of political correctness and taxes. Every innovative idea has come and gone: the nuclear family, the 1950's father, put your baby on his stomach to sleep—wait, no, now it's her side—wait, now it's his back... uh-oh, we're back to the stomach.

As you know, I had five kids over a period of fifteen years. (I don't know if I'm bragging or complaining.) I'm so confused at what's best for them. It's a good thing I didn't know some of the things about childcare my eldest daughter knows now. But wait a few years and things will be different. Again. She tells me her son is to lie on his back to sleep. Her next one will more than likely be told to sleep on his side.

Here are some other gems from the recent past:

An apple a day keeps the doctor away—no, wait, studies have shown that eating an apple every day for bleep years causes cancer.

A glass of wine at night is not good for you—wait, it is good for you... hold on, no it's not good for you. Oh, my bad, it is good for you.

Antibacterial soap is good for you because you kill all the germs—wait, if you kill all the germs, your child's immune system can't grow to overcome them, thus making them allergy prone, making the overuse of antibacterial products bad.

Anyway, you get my drift.

Tangent: Comedian George Carlin once said he heard saliva causes cancer, but not to worry...only if swallowed in small amounts over a long period of time.

I (like so many others) cannot wait for this PC shtuff to go the way of moon sticks. Do you remember those? They were great, weren't they? Tootsie-roll consistency in a long, protein-packed roll. They were food for our astronauts and came out about the same time as Tang. Tang prevailed, but these little edible rolls of goodness went away, and I can't even remember their correct name.

Political Correctness has overstayed its welcome. Time to go now. Has anyone seen its coat?

The thing is, an overwhelming percentage of American people are bone-tired of putting up with this fungus taking over our sensibilities. It seems there's nothing we can do.

John Wayne was quoted as saying, "Don't let the bastards get you down." Problem is, the PC Bastards are bringing us down including themselves, and they don't even know it. The commonsense-less idiots think Legos cause capitalism, coffee needs to be labeled as containing caffeine (that's a short ingredient label), peanuts need to be banned from life, and a host of other opinions relating to ethanol, electric cars, greenhouse effect, global warming, laptops for children of third-world countries... I could go on all day.

I listened to Dennis Miller again the other day—I wish we were related and I might pretend we are. Anyway, he basically stated he has many rituals and preferences, but if he were to walk around town in his skivvies as he likes to do at home, he'd be arrested.

Religious factions want us to put foot baths in public places. Where is the separation of church and state there? It's not a cultural thing. If your culture needs to wash your feet, then wash them and wear suitable shoes for the environment in which you find yourself—when in Rome... By doing so, your feet won't require constant bathing. Oh, my ideas aren't PC? Why not? Why doesn't everyone bow to my beliefs? Work with me here. Aren't I worthy of being a faction of society?

For instance, less than two percent of the entire world's population has peanut allergies. They seemingly want to hang those who don't by their short hairs because they believe the rest of society is secretly trying to kill them off.

Parent of a peanut-allergy child, allow me to ask you something. If your child were allergic to shellfish or milk instead of peanuts, would you still be working so hard to ban peanuts from our schools? Yet, you insist a vast majority of the population bend over for your beliefs and wants *de jour*.

Today you ban peanuts; tomorrow you'll insist my child not receive a higher grade than yours, because, alas, your poor darling cannot handle the stress.

Then, after you get that taken care of, there'll be another cause for you to champion: taking away the rights of others around you, because, darn it, you're just more specialler than they are.

That reminds me. My car insurance went up because my car can withstand a greater impact than most, and my insurance company may have to pay to fix your car if we're in an accident and it's my fault...which is unlikely as I've never been in a car accident where I was behind the wheel (knock on wood). I drive a Subaru. You drive a Saturn. My car is built to withstand accidents. Your car is built to crumble under pressure—but 'green' so, yay you. I'm required to pay for your choice in plastic. Ironically, if you hit me and it's your fault your insurance company has to fix my damages—which will probably be next to nil.

And that's why I pay more for your inability to choose a safe and efficient mode of transportation.

You gotta love PC America.

Baby Pills for Our Babies

I watched a morning show on television, where they had some dudes discussing prescribing birth control pills to our girls in junior high.

I don't completely know how I feel about that yet. But here are some of my initial thoughts.

Haven't there been studies showing 'the pill' causes cancer, especially in women (and in this case, I use the term lightly) who smoke? And we've been told our kids are smoking as young as nine now. I *know*. Some people say they're having sex that young, too. I don't know if I want to believe that.

Aren't you only supposed to take birth control for no more than ten years? So, when they're twenty-one, what?

Sure, it keeps the kids from being parents (and ironically keeps the parents from being parents). But it also (this is where my mind goes to the Stephen-King-side of the realm of things that go bump in the night) keeps the pedophile parent from worrying about fathering his own grandchild.

And it puts the onus and responsibility on the female, much like the vaccination that's supposed to take care of twenty-five percent of the human papillomavirus (HPV), which is the virus girls get from having sex with boys, the virus that can cause Pelvic Inflammatory Disease (PID) and then cervical cancer in some females.

My first three children were born in the one percent, meaning I was on birth control when I found out they were obstinate zygotes. And they have yet to follow my wishes.

Voila! Three kids under five years of age. The pill was sup-posed to be ninety-nine percent accurate, but supposed-to-be doesn't always be.

Why don't we clip the boy? You know, reversible vasec-tomy? Or medically castrate him? I hear the male of the species has a sex drive twenty thousand times greater (calm yourself; I exaggerated for effect) than us poor, frustrated women. Of course, I don't believe it for a second. We women are just so much more sophisticated and demure. And we've been told our entire lives good girls aren't supposed to engage in it...until we're at least engaged, that is. So isn't it *his* responsibility to make sure *his* gift isn't one that keeps on giving? (Don't get up on your high horse. Much of what I write is tongue-in-cheek. And since I have five girls, I have a different and biased point of view here.)

But back to school programs, these are our children. Do we want the schools to administer birth control pills without our knowledge when they already have the right to distrib-ute condoms?

I think handing our burdens to the schools regarding what our kids eat and what they watch and what prescriptions they take and the morals, values, and concepts we want them to learn is irresponsible.

I remember one person said she wanted the school to teach her child how to survive in this world. I disagree with her wants. I want the school to teach my child the three Rs: Reading, wRiting, and aRithmetic

By the way, I still use that mnemonic my second-grade teacher taught me to help me learn how to spell the word arithmetic, which—come to think of it—is probably socially unacceptable now. *A Red Indian Thought He Might Eat Toast In Church.* She taught me to spell. She didn't teach me tol-erance. That was a job for my parents.

On the flip side, some kids can't go to their parents to do the "right" thing by getting on the pill if they want to have sex.

Allow me to clarify. I don't think it's either right or wrong to go on the pill. Not my call if your child is doing this. I only worry about mine. Not because I'm a heartless bitch, but because I'm only responsible for mine, and your values aren't the same as mine. So how dare I impose my beliefs and values on what you want for your child? I wouldn't want you to impose yours on us.

Maybe it's more about teaching our girls to think for themselves and not be pressured into having sex.

Maybe they shouldn't be exposed (no pun intended) so early to the joys of sex.

I know if someone handed me a condom in junior high, I would've looked at it and thought something like, "Why are they putting balloons in wrappers now?"

But that was a hundred years ago. Things were much different then.

The Games People Play

I like the commercials lately showing how inept and non-conforming we are if we choose to write a check or pay cash for an item. Now I see the latest brain-washing fad is putting credit cards in old standby games like LIFE and newer games (I don't know their names). What is the impetus, people? Do we really want our six- to twelve-year-olds learning the joys of credit card debt? Do these games charge a sixteen-to-twenty percent interest every turn on their next turn, compounding interest turn-ly until every player runs out of money and files for bankruptcy by the middle of the game before they reach their goals?

Do they teach our children the best way to have what we want is to pay for everything with cash up-front and leave the loan-sharking to the mobs?

My friend thinks the powers that be (TPTB) are trying to turn our society into a digital finance and information society, wherein the government can track our spending, earning, and living. I don't know if I completely disagree. I remember in the 1980s there was talk of implanting a chip in our hands to keep track of all our information: wealth, employment, identification, health, etc. People put up such a stink. Now we have implants for our pets. And we have all our information on the magnetic strips or chips on our bank, ID, and credit cards. Is it really that far-fetched a dermo-implant is far behind? The key chain credit card where you swipe and go is easy to lose, right? So, don't you believe their next move might be to "offer" the implant for your protection?

What better way to get the next generation to conform to credit spending than credit card games?

I've heard some faction in Seattle, Washington recently passed a bill or law or something banning Legos. Their reasoning was Legos teach children the evils of capitalism. My question is: If this is true, if they did ban Legos for that reason, why didn't they ban Monopoly or like games, instead of just adding credit cards to the rules?

What gives anybody the right to ban anything, anyway? I did wake up in the United States of America this morning, didn't I?

When did the Pledge of Allegiance change to: with liberty and justice for all who conform or are illegal immigrants or who victimize others or who can afford the best lawyers or whoever the ACLU (wait, I mean the CLU - they stopped looking out for America years ago) decides to make a poster child of the week?

Speaking of Seattle and other like communities, y'all will pay four to eight dollars for a cup of coffee and bitch about having to pay three dollars a gallon at the gas pump. At those prices (we'll say five dollars for estimating), figuring sixteen cups per gallon, you pay eighty dollars per gallon for coffee. Wow! (I'm being a hypocrite here, because I do, too: buy coffee at five dollars a cup and bitch about paying three dollars a gallon at the pump. Guilty as charged.)

So I think the question we have to ask ourselves is this: Is it more important to us to pay three dollars a gallon to get to work via vehicle, or eighty dollars a gallon to actually *get to work* once we're there?

Maybe someday someone will ban thinking and you won't need to ask yourselves any questions.

The Web of Life

...is closing in

On us spiders.

We wove it ourselves

And now

We

Are being drug into

A timeless pit,

So carefully built

There's no way out.

The more we climb,

The more we weave,

Blocking out spiders

Behind us

And killing all

Our chances

Of survival.

~age 17 (1979)

Sorry I Blew Up

I attended class last night at the same venue it has been for the past two weeks.

As I'm a creature of habit, I got there a bit early. It takes about two, sometimes three or more—depending on traffic—hours to drive up there and didn't want to get stuck in Denver traffic during rush hour.

So I walked into the building and headed directly for the classroom (which they previously held on the third floor) via the elevator, my mind preoccupied with an RV that almost ran me over on I-25. The car in front of me stopped short. I stopped. The RV struggled to go from seventy-five miles per hour to zero in two seconds. Yikes!

It succeeded; I lived.

Anyway, I boarded the elevator, still lost in thought, and pushed number three (for the third floor). As the elevator started to rise, I looked around a bit. I noticed a menu of activities posted on the wall of the tiny, mobile room.

Huh. John McCain. Isn't that odd? Some guy with the same name as a presidential candidate is speaking at this building sometime tonight. Weird.

The door opened and I stepped out of the elevator to a roomful of black-suited individuals, female and male—all standing around tables looking self-important and more equal than others. (I think I walked in on them patting each other on the back, or something.)

Dressed in blue jeans and a pink sweater, I was *way* out

of place. I nodded politely at their presence, and then headed toward the hallway which led directly to the classroom I'd been attending for the past two weeks.

A rather formidable woman in a black pantsuit held out her hands in a "Hold on there, Sparky" way and said, "This area is secure."

I thought to myself: *define secure.*

I said, "No, that's okay. I'm attending a class around the corner." And I pointed in the general direction.

Pantsuit says, "No! This whole area—this whole floor— is secure."

I thought, *Not so much, I just walked off the elevator... no problems there. How flippin' secure is that? Again: define secure.*

I said, "Oh," and I'm sure I stood there like a deer out of water. Then I said, "They must have moved my class."

I started to get back onto the "secured" elevator to leave those self-important people to smell each other's armpits. Another lady walked me to the doors and said, "Here, let me help you."

I said, "I don't need an escort. I can figure this out. But thank you."

She pushed button number one and walked out of the elevator. I looked closer at the list and saw my class had moved to the second floor that evening.

I said, "Well, thanks, but I needed the second floor..." as the door shut on my words.

Secure.

...And to think I considered voting for McCain.

Now That Was Close

Did I ever tell you of the time I saw a UFO? It was back in the summer of 1972 (stop with the math) and I was sleeping outside under the stars in a sleeping bag with my brother. Let me be clear. He had his own sleeping bag. Anyhoo, I awoke before dawn, but the light of the sun below the horizon illuminated the morning sky, emitting an eerie, not-quite-there feeling. Directly above us floated an object which filled the pre-dawn sky.

It hovered above us at quite a distance, but totally engulfed the sky—creating the optical illusion it levitated merely an arms-length away. Deafeningly quiet, it felt as if it vibrated within. It shone in a gray-silver metallic hue. It seemed multidimensional, in that the underside—the part revealed to me—displayed angles and crevices, much like an engine block. Not circular by any means, it was more of a rectangular crystal made of metal, multi-surfaced with no rhyme or reason to the pattern. No marks, no writing, no lettering of any kind that I could see—it remained over us until the sun peeked over the horizon, then blipped away so fast it seemed to disappear. But I watched it go.

I was frozen in surrealistic stupor more than fear but then finally turned to my brother and asked, "What was that?"

His face told me what my face probably said to him. If we were any older, we might have said WTF, but we didn't use the F word or initials back then. I don't know if the acronym was invented yet. I wonder if whoever invented

WTF gets a royalty every time someone uses it. They'd be a gazillionaire by now, thanks to the entertainment industry, but I'm tangent-ing.

I have no idea what I saw that morning. I've not seen anything like it before or since, even in depictions of others' sightings. I know it wasn't my imagination or a dream. I just know it was.

I recounted the preceding in order to tell you the following:

I was recently abducted by aliens.

I have a hard time admitting this. People will think I'm crazy; a whack job even. But seriously, I was scared.

I had no way of getting away.

I didn't know where they had taken me

...And I can't speak Spanish.

Today,

I caught myself

Remembering

Your smile

So sunny

Your eyes

So bright

Your touch

So gentle

Your love

Now gone.

~ age 16 (1978)

Just Another Day

Originally published in the Military Writers' Society of America's 2014 Anthology

26 May 2014

Hey, You.

It's me again. I'm hoping you'll smile when you read this. At least, I imagine you smiling, holding the envelope in your hands—I miss that smile; the one which lights up your eyes when something tickles or touches you. Damn, I miss you. I miss the smell of you, your chuckle, your dry sense of humor, but mostly that damned infectious smile. The memory of your smile has gotten me through quite a few rough spots, for which I am grateful.

I know I haven't written to you in a while, and for that, I'm sorry. A lot has been happening here, if that's any excuse.

The sewer backed up a couple of months ago. All the pipes from here to the sidewalk needed to be replaced. 'They' told me the pipes were almost a hundred years old. Nothing short of a nightmare, I finally got it worked out. Then, in April, the Colorado winds decided our roof needed replaced... so, now we have a new roof. I hope you like slate gray, because that's the color I picked.

Our old Subaru finally gave out its last bit of energy. Even you have to admit, twenty years is a long time to own a car. Our new car carried a hefty price tag, but as I have no mechanical abilities I did something which will make you cringe—I bought it new—yes, brand-spanking new. Yes, I am aware it lost half its value when I drove it off the lot. To be quite frank, I've no energy to play the sales games anymore. You can chastise me when you get home, regardless, we now own a brand new, blue Subaru Forester.

I hate when men talk to me like I'm an idiot. It's annoying, but I recall what you said about telling them you'll be back, and if they don't do right by us they'll be receiving a visit from you. It's getting more difficult saying that and sounding believable, though. I shouldn't have to hide behind a man for other men to be decent, that's all I'm saying. Thank you for never treating me like an idiot.

Remember how you fell in love with this old house when we first walked onto the porch? You said we'd spend a lot of time fixing it up and turning it into a home in which we'd grow old together. You weren't wrong about the fixing-up part. It feels like I manage to divert one catastrophe when another comes down the pike. It's exhausting some days. I'm not complaining, mind you. This is me being honest. It's hard toeing this line alone, but no worries. I'm holding down the fort as best I can.

On a positive note, I'm making us a little backyard sanctuary of sorts, for when you return. It's a nice place to read and enjoy a glass of wine. I find myself sitting out there more often these days. My mind always drifts to memories of you, and that smile of yours. The fruitless cherry tree you planted when we first moved in has grown so much it provides me with wonderful shade from the afternoon sun.

And my love, I have to tell you—the blossoms carry such a sweet fragrance you can almost taste the sugar in the air; our own slice of paradise. You're gonna love it.

Sarah and Josh officially announced to everyone they're getting married. You remember me telling you about Josh, right? He and Sarah have been together about five years now. They met when she went on her senior trip to Six Flags, and he was there on leave. I told you a while ago I thought he was the one for her. Can I now tell you I told you so?

I told you so.

They were planning an October wedding. They've decided to get married by the judge now that Josh deploys in July. Honestly, I was looking forward to planning big wedding, you know? To occupy my mind a bit? Sarah decided she couldn't go through with a big wedding. There we were, smack dab in the middle of trying on wedding gowns and she bursts into tears. When I got her calmed down she told me she wanted no one but you to walk her down the aisle, and she most certainly had no desire to do it alone. I told her we understood, and that we'd back her whatever her decision.

You'd be so proud of her. She graduated last week—top honors—with a degree in Early Childhood Development. At first she wasn't keen on participating in the graduation ceremony. I talked her into it by telling her you'd be there in spirit—took some pretty good pictures of her, too, if I do say so myself. I'll stick them in with this letter. Your daughter's grown into such a beautiful and accomplished woman—like we'd always hoped she'd be. I see so much of you in her, and yes, she has your smile. It's so hard to believe it's been ten years. She was only twelve when they told us you disappeared in Iraq, and no one knew where or how you were.

Watching our daughter grow from that awkward preteen into the beautiful woman who took her place has been both heartache and a blessing. I've been able to witness her growth, all the while knowing how much you're missing; knowledge that only widens the chasm of emptiness in my chest.

I yearn for your touch; your strong, safe arms around me, my love. I am surrounded by your memory—the smell of coffee brewing in the morning, hearing our song on the radio, the wine glass you chipped right before you left... and that damned cherry tree.

Your shirts wait in our closet for you, although they forgot your scent years ago. Framed faces seem to mock me as I pass, for I see new wrinkles appearing around my eyes and lips almost daily while your face remains the same—on our walls and in my memory. I wonder if you'll still want me. I wonder if you'll even recognize me. But mostly, I wonder where you are, and I wonder if you're okay. I keep sending these letters even though they keep getting returned... unopened. Seems silly, I know.

I've spent every day of the last ten years thinking you're going to show up on our doorstep, unannounced. The days have turned into years. I wonder why I still hold on to hope. Then, I think 'today could be the day they find you and bring you home.' So I'll place this letter in an envelope. I'll put a 'Forever' stamp in the corner, and I'll address it the way I always do. I'll seal it with a kiss, and send it out on a wavering thread of stubborn hope that maybe this time it'll find you, and this time you'll read my words. And you'll smile. And you'll be reminded we so much love and miss you and want you back. And somehow, this time, you'll find some way to come back home to us.

God speed, my love. You've been gone far too long.

All my love, forever and always,
Me

You Think That I'm in Love?

You think that I'm in love? Hah!

Oh, silly, silly you.

For if I were in love

These things I'd do for you:

I'd snuggle up beside you

And tell you all I think

Then I'd nibble on your ear,

And, for you, I'd try to wink.

I'd wash your dirty clothes

And the dishes in the sink.

I'd even rise at midnight

To get yourself a drink.

I'd clean up all your messes,

And rub your neck for kinks.

I'd even sweep or wax the floor

And never raise a stink.

I'd worry when you're sick:

'Feed a fever? Starve a cold?'

And stay close beside you

Until you're gray and old! (ugh!)

I'd write you mushy letters,

And silly, little rhymes.

When I said 'good-bye' to you

I'd kiss you twenty times.

If you e'er came home too late,

It'd worry me to tears.

I'd have trouble keeping down

My buried thoughts and fears.

But ne'er need you worry,

I'd said it once to you

I'd do those silly things

That lovers often do.

I'd do all that for nothing

If, for one minute it was true.

I'd do all that, and so much more

If I really did love you.

~ age 16 (1978)

Being Soul in America

CNN did a program called *Being Black In America*. I'm not going to comment on that except to say we all had our problems growing up. We all had our crosses to bear. All of our ancestors had some kind of difficulty to overcome.

Pain is colorblind; suffering isn't specific. Whether or not you want to say, "Yeah, but mine was worse," or "You had it easier, and still do," nobody knows what it's like to be anyone else.

I grew up in a small country town, where everybody knew everybody else. And they all knew everyone's business, or so they thought. But if everyone knew what was really going on in my little town, behind our closed doors, they never let it show they knew my father was a monster... and *the* Boy Scout master in town. I often wonder how many little boys he "scouted." But I'm going off on a tangent, here. Let me get back to my thoughts.

The American culture is full of people as diverse as creatures in a pond—and it's one we're losing fast. We all see the differences. We all see the similarities. Why do we have to keep hashing out what one group sees as incongruities and another sees as opportunities?

There are a few in every crowd who need their brains removed for the common good, people who think the color of your skin means anything at all. It doesn't. Just because you're dark-skinned doesn't mean you're treated badly by society, and just because you're light-skinned doesn't mean you aren't. ...and every shade in between.

We're becoming a culture of Hyphen-Americans. We no longer have a culture in which to be proud, it seems. Our forefathers' visions are now jokes to touchy-feely Hyphen-Americans.

A man can brutally rape a child, and the Supreme Court says capital punishment doesn't fit his crime. What would? Should Yeti brutally rape and assault him?

Turn the other cheek? An eye for an eye? Let this generation pay for the crimes of our ancestors? Who are we supposed to pay back? How long will we have to pay for the decisions of our great-great-grandfathers? How or how much will we have to pay?

When will it ever be enough?

I cannot wait for the day Americans stand side by side and say, "I love this country, and not because my husband has a chance at being president, but because I have been afforded every opportunity my grandparents and great-grandparents weren't. But through their sacrifices and hard work I am who I am today. And I am grateful to this country and my God—whomever I perceive my God, if any, to be—and to all who came and struggled before me. I will do my best to make the next generation better than the last one. I promise to leave this country a better place than when I arrived. And I will stop placing blame on others and start utilizing the challenges placed before me as a learning/building block to spring forth to my horizons, my life, my destiny."

Yes, I had a monster for a father. Yes, my upbringing was in poverty and shame. But wonder upon wonders, I now have a treasure chest of experiences from which to draw as I take pen in hand and do what I love to do: write.

I give thanks daily for that monster, who was instrumental in making me who I am today, not unlike the people who loved and cherished me. Because of him I have more compassion and strength and understanding. There's no sense wishing I'd received those lesson in a more loving environment, because hey, you take what you're given and you carve a life for yourself. You surround yourself with love and lovely people.

And you thank the Universe daily for this wonderful opportunity of being Soul in America.

The Burdens We Carry

Amy became aware she was no longer in her bed.

She stood on a plateau of gray nothingness. Around her stood people of all different shapes and sizes, but all were charcoal gray from head to toe.

Even their clothing appeared colorless.

She was taken in by the vastness of the plateau and the infinite number of people she saw.

Amy looked down at herself.

She, too, echoed the monochrome of the others, her skin as dull as the garment she wore.

The people looked ahead with anticipation on their faces. Amy's eyes followed theirs, and feelings of wonder and hope overcame her when she saw a glow on the horizon. Her heart beat faster and she had the urge to run as fast as she could toward the source of the beacon.

Amy took a step forward and felt a heavy weight upon her back. She noticed when others took that first step forward, a brightly colored bag appeared on their backs. The others grabbed the opening of the bag as it slung over their shoulders and trudged—burdened, but blissful—toward the beautiful horizon.

"How can they walk with such pressure?" Amy thought. "I wonder what it is."

She removed the bag from her shoulder, pleased to see it was yellow. She always enjoyed the color yellow.

A golden cord kept the contents from spilling out, but

Amy had no problem opening the bag. She peered inside and saw glowing bricks of gold. She picked one up. No, it wasn't real gold of earthly fame. It was merely a heavy golden brick. And man, it was a burdensome load.

Amy began to cry.

A man walking by stopped to the sound of her sobs.

"Please, miss, don't cry. Is there anything I can do to help?"

"I don't know you, do I?" Amy asked through her tears.

The man put down his brilliant blue bag and held out his hand.

"My name is Paul. Tell me, what can I do to help? You seem so lost and afraid."

"I am afraid. You see, I have all these bricks to carry, and I'm unsure if I can do it. I'm so afraid I won't make it. I feel so alone."

"Would it help if I carried that brick for you? Would it lessen your burden?"

"Yes, Paul, I think it might."

Amy handed the brick to Paul and as their skin touched a feeling of love and security washed over her. Her heart felt less heavy as Paul opened his bag and placed Amy's brick on the top.

As he closed the bag, Paul looked at Amy with love and gratitude.

"It pleases me to have helped you, miss. Thank you for allowing it."

"Thank you, Paul," Amy said, as she picked up her own bag, flung it over her shoulder, and started toward the light.

She had walked quite a bit before the bag felt burdensome once again. She looked ahead at the light, which didn't seem to be getting any closer. Despair washed over her. Amy sat down and started crying once more.

An old lady passing by stopped and sat down next to Amy.

"My dear child, you look distraught. Please, tell me

what's wrong."

"Oh, it's nothing. I don't mean to hold you up, ma'am. Please, continue on your way."

"Friends call me Mabel...'cause it's my name, you see," said Mabel. "Now you just wipe those tears from that pretty little face of yours and come out with it. I needed to sit a spell any old how."

Amy wiped her face with the back of her hand. She looked at the old woman sitting in front of her. Mabel wore deep caverns in her face from years of life and love. Her watery eyes held a story of their own.

"It's just ...I don't think I can make it. I feel so desperate and the way is so far. I want so much to continue, but it is just too much."

"Oh, is that all? Well, why didn't you say so?" Mabel reached over and opened Amy's yellow bag. She took the top brick and placed it into her own scarlet bag.

"That should help," she said. And with a swift motion, Mabel swung her own bag onto her back and resumed her walk toward the horizon.

Amy stood and picked up her yellow bag, which was considerably lighter. She thought she could make it now. In fact, she knew she could.

It wasn't long before Amy's bag began to dig into her back. She stopped walking at once and threw the bag down. How was she ever supposed to achieve her goal if things kept happening to her? She became incensed. Why did she have to deal with this? Why her? Nobody else looked like they were in pain. She looked around at the other souls making the way toward her goal—*her* reward.

"It's not fair!" she screamed into the crowd.

People stopped and gaped at her.

"Don't look at me that way!" she shouted. "You people have no right to walk without pain. Look at me. Look at my pain. You have no right. I tell you, it's not fair!"

A little boy held out his hand to Amy. "Give me what causes you pain," he said. "I am young. I can handle it."

Amy was so angry she threw her brick at him, but in one deft movement the boy caught the brick and tucked it neatly away in his purple bag and smiled.

"Thank you," he said as he continued on his way.

But Amy still steamed with anger. She wanted to punch someone. Anyone. Then she felt a warm hand upon her shoulder. Amy turned around.

A kindly old man stood with his hand outstretched. "That much anger will make a soul sour. You need to relieve yourself of it. Come on, hand it over before your heart turns to stone and all hope is gone."

Amy dutifully grabbed the topmost brick and handed it to the man in silence. Her anger dissipated. Her heart felt light once more. The pain in her body disappeared. She was ready to continue.

Amy picked up her bag and noticed there were only three bricks left. Her burden felt lighter, manageable even. She might be able to make it to her goal so very soon.

She swung the bag on her back and practically skipped on her way, leaving other souls in her wake.

But as she passed them, she began to notice something strange. The people walking along beside her—the people she hurried past—glowed with a soft yellow light. She looked down at her own skin.

It answered back in monochrome.

Amy looked far ahead and saw the souls way up there almost beamed with golden light—much like the horizon. She stopped in her tracks.

Maybe something was wrong. Maybe she should be turning golden, too. Maybe she'd walked too fast and hadn't given the light ahead a chance to soak through her skin.

"Is anything wrong?"

Amy turned to see a woman about her own age standing a few feet away.

"Um, no. I don't think so, anyway. I was just...I was thinking maybe I should have walked slower. Maybe I didn't do this the right way. What do you think?"

The woman looked toward the golden horizon. Amy noticed a golden glow emitting from the woman's skin. She felt a pang of jealousy. The woman looked into Amy's eyes and smiled.

"I know what you're thinking," she said. "You have doubts about your trip, about your destination, about your origination. You also feel you should be this golden color...that you deserve to glow, too."

"How do you know that?" Amy asked.

"Because I feel that way, too. I have doubts and moments of jealousy. But I think I've figured out a way to work through these thoughts." The woman held out her hand to Amy. "Please let me help you."

Amy reached in her bag and handed two bricks to her. Amy felt gratitude for this stranger who wanted to share her burden. After the woman placed Amy's bricks into her own green bag, Amy leaped forward and hugged the woman fiercely.

"Thank you ever so much. You have been such a blessing to me," Amy said.

"And thank you, Amy. I've always been here to help you."

"How did you know my name?" Amy looked deep into the eyes of the woman standing before her and recognized her sister, Beth.

Beth smiled and said, "Now, go. You have much ground to cover." She kissed Amy on the cheek.

Amy's heart overflowed as she left her sister. She took her yellow bag with only one brick and ran as fast as she could toward her goal. She passed people along the way who stood crying about their own burdens.

Amy felt no pity. She watched as others ran to these poor souls' sides to assist in their loads.

Amy had no time for that. Her goal was so close.

So very, very close.

Amy came to a tower of golden beams—the most beautiful thing she had ever seen. She wanted so much to enter. Then her heart lurched when she realized it held nothing of tangible substance. Only light.

She turned and looked out over the crowd of souls headed her way.

A man walked up beside her, his own bag brimming with burdens, his skin too brilliant to see. She watched as he opened his bag and poured gray sand on the ground. She saw him throw his orange bag far into the air. Amy sucked in her breath as the orange bag disappeared into the vastness above. She covered her mouth in awe as the man disappeared into the golden tower—becoming one with the light of the goal.

Amy looked into her own bag. The solitary brick inside continued to glow. It had yet to turn to gray sand.

A woman beside Amy busily poured sand from her own bag.

"Excuse me." Amy cleared her throat and continued. "Please forgive, but do you know why I'm not golden? Why hasn't my brick turned to sand? What have I done wrong?"

"Oh, that's silly. You can't do anything wrong, child," the woman said. "Here, let me see."

The woman looked into Amy's bag. "Well, dear, wherever are your bricks?"

Amy pointed into the crowd. "I gave my bricks to them."

"Oh, I see. Paul has your FEAR. See, he's struggling under its weight...no, wait. See? He's overcome your FEAR." The woman sighed in relief.

Amy watched as Paul stood straighter and glowed brighter.

The woman looked around some more.

"There now, I see you've given your DESPAIR over to

Mabel. What a wonderful woman she is, don't you think? Full of life and vigor...a real down-to-earth woman, she is. Wait. I think your DESPAIR may have done her in...No. Great! WAY TO GO, MABEL. KEEP ON TRUCKING! See, my dear, nothing to fret. Mabel had her own DESPAIR to overcome first, and then she handled yours with ease."

The woman finished emptying the sand from her bag. She rolled the bag into a ball and prepared to toss it into the sky.

"No, wait, please." Amy was mesmerized by the glow Mabel now emitted and wondered at the calm look on Mabel's face as she walked toward them.

"What dear?" The woman lowered her hands, still holding her bag.

"Please...more," was all Amy could muster. Her heart raced and she felt she may have made a big mistake.

"All right, then, if I have to show you from A to Zed— we all have our burdens to carry. To you, yours look worse than mine. But look at that woman there." She pointed at a young woman walking toward the light. "Her burdens were the same as yours, but her FEAR, DESPAIR, ANGER...well, all of them actually—stemmed from cancer. Look at the little boy who took your PAIN. His burdens stemmed from child abuse by the people he loved."

Amy searched the crowd and found the boy on his back. His mouth opened in a silent scream. His eyes watered with tears and his body writhed in pain.

"Oh my God. No, I didn't mean...but he wanted it. He asked to take my pain. He thanked me for it."

"Didn't they all?" The woman smiled. "Just because one offers, dear, doesn't make it okay to burden others with your load. Now look at the old man to whom you unloaded your ANGER."

Amy had a difficult time taking her eyes from the little boy, who was now curled up in a ball and rocking back and forth on the gray, unforgiving ground.

She pulled her eyes away and searched the crowd for the old man. She not as much saw him as heard him. His angry voice carried over the crowd.

"Get out of my way, you ignorant fool! What do you mean you don't agree with me? How dare you think you know anything, you ignoramus!"

The man sat on his bag and shook his fists at others. Hatred blazed across his face. A small girl walked up to the old man and handed him a brick from her bag. The old man stopped shouting, put the girl's brick into his bag, and started walking toward them again.

"What just happened?" Amy asked.

"That young child gave the old man her LOVE, the only brick one should ever give away. Because, you see, once you give it another one replaces it in your bag. Look. See? You still have your LOVE, even though you gave it away."

Amy looked in to see the one remaining brick in her bag.

"But why is LOVE a burden?"

"Oh, my dear. You'll have to figure that one out for yourself."

Amy looked out across the crowd, searching for someone. Her eyes rested on a beautiful woman about her own age, sitting on a bag and sobbing pitifully. Amy knew her sister struggled with DOUBT and JEALOUSY. She knew because she had burdened her with them.

Amy looked for the little boy. He stood where he once lay weak and limp, but his skin glowed a little brighter, and a smile crept onto his worn face.

Amy looked at her sister—the goal so close but seemingly giving up.

Amy looked at the woman beside her.

"But I didn't give it away. LOVE, that is."

"Why forever not, dear? It's the only burden you carry worth giving away." The old lady threw her bag into space and joined her light with the others.

Amy stood alone.

And she felt more alone than she stood.

She looked into her bag. Her golden brick taunted her.

She peered out into the crowd. The boy had started walking. She ran to him.

"Hi, lady," he said weakly. "What brings you back here?"

Amy took the brick out of her bag and handed it to the boy, whose face beamed brighter once the brick touched his skin. He placed the brick into his bag and wrapped his arms around Amy's neck.

"You are a kind and wonderful being," he said.

She didn't feel so kind and wonderful, but she hugged him back just the same.

She then ran to her sister.

Amy put her hand into her bag and pulled out another brick. The woman was right. It replaced itself. She handed the brick to Beth.

"I am sorry to have burdened you with my JEALOUSY and DOUBT."

Beth took the brick and smiled at Amy.

"Thank you, Amy. I was sitting here, feeling it was unfair you got to enter first, but now I see you deserve to go first. You are a wonderful and kind person. But I doubt if I'll ever be good enough to enter."

Amy felt her bag. Sure enough, there was another brick in it. She handed this second brick to her sister, who took it. She noticed her sister's skin begin to glow a brighter golden.

Then she noticed something else. Her own skin shone as brightly.

Amy pulled her sister up and took her hand. "Come on, sis—let's go there together."

In Something Like the Fifth Grade...

...there was this guy I really liked. We hung out with our friends at recess and giggled (well, I did) and talked (I guess that was all me, too). But he did smile at me and he stood close by.

One day at recess he asked me to follow him. He led me behind the fifth-grade stairs and into a corner unseen by teachers' eyes and sat on the asphalt.

I was (and am) painfully shy. It took all the bravery I could muster to walk with him.

He gestured for me to sit beside him in the corner between the brick wall and cement stairs. I sat. He timidly reached for my hand. I remember his skin was soft and warm. He leaned in to perhaps kiss me when our friends spied us and started pointing and laughing.

He took off one way, I the other, both of us beet-red and near tears.

Later that day during gym class (back when gym was co-ed and consisted of two days a week of chasing a random ball around the field in our regular clothes), he sidled up next to me and said what I heard as, "What class do we have next?"

I heard my friends giggling behind me, so I said, "I don't KNOW!" But I mumbled the first two words, so it came out more of a "NO!," I fear.

Then I ran away like the brave, confrontational soul I am.

The next day my friend asked me why I told him "no" when he asked me to go with him. I told her I didn't recall him asking me to go with him and I most certainly would not have said "no" to him [insert indignant tone here]—I really liked him. She said he said he had asked me during gym class, and I had screamed out "No!"

At that point I realized what had happened and asked my friend to ask him to ask me again, because in the fifth grade you always ask your friends to do stuff like that. I suppose in high school it's kind of the opposite. You ask your friend to break it to your significant other that he's not so much any more—significant, that is. At least that's how I got jilted as a sophomore. But as usual, I'm digressing. If I could steer you back to my original story...

Too late! I had an enemy for life, it seems. Not only did he stop talking to me, he started making fun of me. But who could blame him, really? I thought he asked me what was up next on our academic agenda. Would it have killed me to say, "Algebra"? Then he might have looked at me like I was eating frog eyeballs and repeated his question. We may have been laughing about it to this day, snuggled on the couch and reminiscing to our grandchildren.

I got a ticket for stopping on my way to work this morning. Or rather, for not stopping...at a four-way stop sign...in which I had a truck in front of me and cars going other directions in the queue. Truck stopped and proceeded. I pulled up to the sign and stopped, waiting for green car to my left to go—as it was his right-of-way. Then, I pulled out and turned right. Cop caught up to me two blocks later, stating I'd not stopped. I have no proof. I know what I know. I know I stopped. If I hadn't, I would've caused an accident.

It'll cost me $110 and four points if I walk away with my tail between my legs. Chances are, if I fight it, I'll still have to pay.

It put me in a really off mood all day.

As I was driving home, grumbling because there are so

many better uses for $110 than to pay some jerk who lies behind a badge, it dawned on me: I had snakes writhing from my forehead and casting black shadows with my dark mood everywhere I went.

Suppose someone—some guy—liked me from afar (I know, stretch, right?) and was watching me at that very moment, wondering if I was worth the pain and embarrassment of asking me what class we had next...

And saw me in that particular state of mind, a state of mind I'm not typically in, by the way, but it doesn't matter. The poison is spread. All he could possibly hear is me screaming "No!"

Life really doesn't give one much of a second chance, does she?

Just Friends

Your hand on the small of my back

pulled me into your embrace.

A good-bye hug between friends

...nothing more.

"Good seeing you again," you said.

Your body pressed fully against mine.

It learned my secrets; traced my valleys.

A veil of modesty;

Layers of material pressed vapor thin kept us divided.

...never before so aware of how thin.

An eternity passed in seconds,

encompassed in your arms; you in mine.

Time wasn't.

This must be what home feels like.

Was it just me?

Or did you feel our connection

when we parted

as friends?

Lonely People

I don't know how to begin this post. It's a touchy subject—loneliness—and subjective at that. I've been sitting here staring at my computer screen, searching for the appropriate words to describe my feelings.

You can live with someone for over a decade and be lonely almost every day of it...4,748 days, each filled with hours of abject loneliness.

No kind words.

All actions and decisions derided or overruled.

Being considered the worst possible version of yourself by the one person who's supposed to love you for better or worse.

Harshest of all, your unsaid words fall upon deaf ears; all communication is lost.

The irony is the person you lived with may have been exceedingly comfortable in the life they forged with you:

Dinner on the table.

Kids and money managed.

Laundry washed, folded, and put away.

House clean and presentable for company.

The choice to come and go as they please, with whomever they wish.

And no one to question their authority...

Their life was really quite nice, I imagine.

I can see why it turned upside down when a less-than had the audacity to leave.

But who's to say being alone is any better?

There's a lady at work who's a bit older than me. She says she thinks no one is content with their life. Those who are married wish they weren't, and those who are single wish they had a partner.

I think she may be onto something.

I'm not alone in my loneliness. I know that, but knowing doesn't ease the ache.

I look around and see loneliness seeping from the pores of people around me. I hear tales of people posting on Internet dating sites, checking out people at the gym, hoping to crash their cart into someone else's cart in the meat aisle of the grocery store.

Undoubtedly, we're all lonely at some point in our lives.

And not merely an "I wish I could find someone to go to the show with" lonely. A real, heart-wrenching, going-to-bed-with-a-chasm-of-an-ache-inside-your-chest lonely. Knowing your heart closed up shop years ago—the last time you had the audacity to leave.

That last guy—the last guy—took a toll on your heart (and self-esteem) you're not willing to accept, and are unable to *not* accept because anything else is just too painful. And if you give love just one more try and it turns out like the last dozen tries, you may not recover.

This time will never be a "this time" because you have no more "next time" left in you. Your heart, quite frankly, can't afford another "this time." Your cup has ceased to overflow and not only depleted, it's got the calcified, chalk-like dust caked in the bottom.

And yet, as lonely as you feel you are, and as much as you know you are, you're not alone in the warehouse of lonely people.

We're all wandering around in our loneliness bubbles, unable and unwilling to reach out to our warehouse-mates because the only thing worse than being hurt by love, or being lonely, is being psuedo-stalked by someone who's taken an interest in you, whom you find totally outside the realm of your criteria ...even though that particular list has dwindled over the years from fourscore non-negotiable items down to "kind, generous, and mentally stable."

I like being alone, for the most part. I like my select group of friends. I adore spending my time in the mountains or on the beach, writing my books, drawing, and indulging in other various forms of artsy-fartsy projects. I'm satisfied with my life...for the most part.

But when the lights go out and my blankets refuse to snuggle, the loneliness creeps under my closed bedroom door and crawls silently into bed with me. My heart sings the sad lullaby of a sorrowful tune.

And then I think how nice it is not to have those same blankets pulled over my head after he farts in bed.

Jeffrey on My Mind

I don't know what made me think of him, but I awoke this morning with Jeffrey on my mind. Jeffrey... Jeff was my brother-in-law, but he was also my friend. At the age of nineteen he decided he'd had enough, and put a rifle to his head.

Life *is* hard for most of us, especially on the dark days when it seems all we have to look forward to is struggle, struggle, struggle, die.

The story goes something like this (and it's been, twenty-some years now so details are sketchy at best): He found out the girl he loved was horribly beaten by an old boyfriend of hers when the old beau discovered she was seeing someone new—Jeff.

Jeff visited her in the hospital, where she told him the beating had aborted Jeff's baby. Apparently he wasn't even aware there *was* a baby until that moment. At the time, Jeff was saving up for an apartment, dishes, towels—stuff like that there, and putting some money aside so he could take classes at the local community college.

It reads like a bad novel, really—certain family members believed going back to school was a monumental waste of money and time. They told him he should spend his time and money on more worthy pursuits.

The girlfriend was released from the hospital, and promptly ran back into the arms of Beau the Beater. Jeff's life started to fall apart. He was flailing in the wind like a well-worn t-shirt on a decrepit clothesline.

On Halloween night of that year, Jeff dressed up like Jesse James and attended a party with his older brother, Scott.

When the alcohol had sufficiently pickled Jeff's brain and the words and tears of despair started flowing, he stated he may as well kill himself. Scott, in some warped-wisdom way told Jeff he didn't believe Jeff could or would do it—Jeff wasn't man enough, apparently.

The note Jeff left said: "I'm a man of my word. Tell Scott he's an asshole."

That's my recollection, anyway. He'd had enough pain, and too much liquor.

I miss him.

Jeff was a beautiful soul, always there to lend a hand or shoulder. I was living in California the night he stopped living. I wish... it's just that *I* have two shoulders, and two hands. I wish he would've reached out to me.

My daughter was a good baby, except when she wasn't. And when she wasn't, she cried all the time. Never stopped. Until she was cradled in her uncle Jeff's arms, that is. He'd sit with her for hours, rocking and singing, and she'd lay there, mesmerized, staring into his face. She awarded him her first smile.

Good kid that Jeff. Funny and smart and kind and patient. But, he'd had enough pain in his life. Who could argue with that? Thinking his child was dead and the woman he loved was back with the man who killed it, Jeff never learned the child was a fantasy of his girlfriend's sick, twisted mind—which apparently it was.

Oh, I suppose he had many other reasons of which I'm unaware—but he took away from me (and the others who loved him dearly) the chance to help him through those reasons. He took away my daughters' uncle.

I miss him—did I mention that? Because he may have had enough of the crap, but we didn't have enough of him.

And, I wonder... Did he really have enough, enough?
Enough warm embraces?
Enough laughter and companionship?
Giggling 'til your sides hurt?
Sunrises and sunsets?
Wishing on falling stars?
Windstorms and rainstorms and soft snow so deep you lose your way?
The taste and warmth of a freshly baked chocolate chip cookie?
Debating with someone worthy into the wee morning hours?
Feeling the cool wind tickle every inch of your body on a warm day?
Or the heat of a campfire warming your toes on a cold one?
Witnessing a spotted fawn struggle to stand?
Or an eagle diving into a lake and emerging clutching a fish?
And the smells... the wonderful, glorious smells of falling rain, cut grass, pine trees, wildflowers—the scents of life?
Enough *Love*? Enough *Life*?
Enough pain? Yeah, I get that. But life is more than pain. Wounds heal and dying's easy. You can do that any time.
Living, on the other hand... living and sensing and feeling and noticing the worthwhile—appreciating the worthwhile— that's the hard part; the most rewarding part.
The whole situation makes me sad. I wish he hadn't been so selfish. I wish he had dressed up as John Wayne that night instead, and heeded that man's immortal words: "Don't let the bastards get you down!"

Jeff would have been about forty now. Instead, he let the bastards win.

Get Over It!

I find it strange humans say "you need to get over it" when someone they care about (or don't) is hurting—for whatever reason. Is there a specific time-line one has to follow in order to "get over it?" Does one get an hour, or a day, or a few years? Do you get a different 'over it' schedule depending on the varying degrees of pain inflicted on your soul?

For instance, how much time is one allotted to get over the death of a loved one? How about the malicious, vindictive, or dishonest words of a virtual stranger? Or the harsh betrayal or abuse from someone close? How about the infidelity and mendacity of a spouse?

I know from experience, it takes as long as it takes. And the strange thing is until you're over it you don't have a clue as to when you'll be over it. One minute you're not, and then something happens. Enough time has passed maybe, or your heart gets a case of Alzheimer's, or you stop caring, and then you're over it. Just like that. Yesterday you had no idea you'd feel differently about your situation today.

Or, maybe you think you're over it and then something happens—like an ex-family member yarns yet another confabulation about you and *WHAM* back to the front of the line! Over it yet? Nope, not so much.

Have you ever been in the situation where your heart was broken by your first serious boyfriend (ever) and a couple of years have passed, and you think you're over it, finally? You haven't seen him in years—and you barely remember anything about him, and then he walks into the room...and your knees buckle, your hands begin to shake, and your heart takes up temporary residence in your throat?

Yeah, not so much over it now, are you?

I tell you what else you never really get over: The smell of your newborn's breath when the nurse brings her bedside to breastfeed; the sound of your baby's first uncontrollable belly-laugh; the apprehension you feel with your toddler's first few tentative steps; the look of wonder on your child's face when she discovers new things; new worlds; new ideas. The feeling consuming your heart the first time your child tells you she loves you—or says you're the best Momma ever (and I think *you're* the best Jack ever).

And the warm, comfortable all-consuming feeling of your love's embrace, his tender kiss and unconditional love—and then you realize you finally understand. You're home, and nothing else matters.

When it doesn't matter anymore—that's when your heart truly starts to heal and you know eventually you'll "get over it." No matter how cynical or jaded you may have become, there's hope on the horizon.

In Sickness

I ache.

I shiver.

I flush cold with fever.

I nestle my shoulder deep

into the warm cave of your armpit.

My heavy head finds soft purchase

in the valley between your shoulder and chest.

Your strong arm tenderly cradles my back.

The cadence of your breath lulls me...

I sleep.

I dream.

I heal in your love.

As the bonds of sleep release me

I slowly awaken

Your arm morphs into my blanket.

I stir.

Your chest reveals itself as my pillow.

I rise.

My shoulder has no cave.

I feel your absence.

You exist only in my dreams.

You've yet to enter my life.

You.

The one

who will snuggle me

in sickness and in health.

Age Less

My oldest friend is eighty-seven, whereas my oldest friend is forty-seven.

My youngest friend is twenty-one, whereas my newest friend is thirty-one.

When I was twenty-one, I felt forty-six without the heart-aches and experiences (and laugh-lines) which come with time.

Now that I'm forty-six, I'm still twenty-one; still wishing on stars, believing in, and hoping for the best.

My face has changed, but old friends recognize me.

My body has changed, but old clothes fit me.

I've not changed. Not really.

Nobody told me hair would start to grow where none did before, and where there was hair, it would begin to fade away—or run wild like kudzu.

No one explained why gray hair is coarser, nails become thicker while skin becomes thinner, and even though your eyesight may dim, your perceptions won't.

When I'm talking with my thirty-one-year-old friend, we feel like equals to me. Yet when I listen to my eighty-seven-year-old friend, I don't notice she's any older than me.

I hear people younger than me complain about their aches and pains. I have none yet.

I hear people older than me brag about their aches and pains, and how much medicine they're on. I'm not on any yet.

It befuddles me when I think of all the time that has passed between twenty-one and forty-six, and yet I don't feel a quarter of a Century older. Smarter? Wiser? Who knows? Doesn't feel like it. I'm not saying I haven't changed at all. It doesn't feel any different from where I sat twenty-five years ago.

In three plus years these fingers will have had half a Century of sand pass through them. Why didn't anyone let me in on the secret of aging?

The Sad Little Tail of Beauregard Buttons

Once upon a time, there was a cute little puppy named Beauregard Buttons. His owners, Jack and Jo, loved Beau with all their hearts. They played with him. They fed and watered him daily. They bathed him weekly. But most of all they snuggled and loved Beau almost every minute of every day.

"Look at his little tail." They laughed. "Look how it wiggles and wags."

Beau was a quick little tyke full of energy and life. He liked to run and play and jump. He liked to chase.

Jo and Jack let Beau play inside the fenced yard around his lovely home as much as possible, because they knew he was safe and he so much loved to run.

One day as Beau was chasing a beautiful blue butterfly across the lawn, it led him to the gate and out onto the sidewalk.

Beau stood still and looked around this open and new world. He looked back at the gate. Someone must have left it open. He started to go back in.

The blue butterfly swirled around Beau's head once more, capturing his attention, and led him playfully down the dangerous street, away from his home with Jack and Jo.

Jack looked outside and saw the open gate. She ran through the yard calling to Beau. Soon Jo came out to help. They ventured out into the street, calling his name.

"Beau! Buttons! Where are you? Here, boy."

There was no sign of their little doggie anywhere.

The girls called the police. They called the pound. They called Grammie to drive around town and look for their puppy, but alas...no Beau. No Beau anywhere.

Jack and Jo went to bed that night, crying and wishing they'd checked the gate more often.

The next day, as Jo and Jack were getting ready for school, they heard a knock on the door.

Standing on their doorstep was a stout, homely woman with pitted skin and a mop of dirty blonde hair piled atop her head. She held out a card. Jo took it.

It read CANINE PROTECTION SERVICES ~ JESSICA WALTERS.

"We have your dog," she snipped with a snarl. "He's safe now, but we've taken him into protective custody. He ran away; therefore, we find you neglectful."

She shoved another paper in the girls' faces.

"You'll report to this court, at this time, to answer to these serious charges."

Ms. Walters turned around and exited the porch like an ogre going back under its bridge.

Jo looked at Jack.

Jack looked at Jo.

They both looked at the card.

They didn't know what to say. They didn't know what to do. No one asked them what had happened. No one told them what to do next. But most important of all, no one told them where Beauregard Buttons was, or if he was okay.

The day came when Jo and Jack appeared in front of the judge.

"This is your public defender," the judge told them.

"Don't say a word," the public defender warned them.

"In the best interest of the puppy," Ms. Walters reminded them.

"Guilty!" declared the judge.

And court was over before Jo and Jack knew what happened.

Meanwhile...

Beau sat all alone in the corner of a small trashy house. He was surrounded by dirty sad dogs and big mean dogs. They looked at him and snarled.

"Lookit the new kid. What a loser," the bully-dog said.

When food was served, bully-dog pushed Beau aside. Beau went to bed hungry and lonely.

One day, the frumpy cold woman named Bertha, who owned the home in which Beau was staying, snatched him up and headed out the door.

"Are we going home? Did you find Jo and Jack?" Beau wagged his tail and hoped Bertha would answer.

She didn't.

He watched out the window as house after house flew by. At one point he thought he saw his home and started barking. "Stop! Stop!"

Bertha swatted him. "Shush!"

They pulled up to a stark building with a tall chain-link fence. Bertha got out and carried Beau inside. Beau was frightened. Where was he headed now? It didn't smell friendly. It didn't feel friendly.

He looked up and saw Jo and Jack. He watched them smile as they saw him. Beau ran to them.

Jo and Jack dropped to their knees and petted and loved and snuggled Beau just like old times.

"Oh! You love me! I knew you wouldn't forget about me," Beau said.

Beau wiggled and squirmed and licked at their faces and noses and nibbled at their hair.

What a wonder. They had found each other again. Beau promised himself he'd never wander away again.

"Come on, guys. Let's go." Beau barked as he wiggled and wagged toward the door, looking over his shoulder and begging them to come. "Come on. Take me home."

But Jo and Jack didn't follow.

They called him back and played some more until Bertha walked in and said time was up.

She picked up Beau and said, "Say good-bye."

"No," Beau whined.

"No!" He cried.

"No, no, no, no, no!" He whimpered and struggled against her strong grasp, as Bertha walked out with Beau over her shoulder. He kept looking back at Jo and Jack.

"I know you want me," he said. "I see you crying. I promise I'll be good from now on. Please don't make me go. Please don't let her take me. It's not nice there. They're mean to me. I promise I'll be good."

All the way back to Bertha's house, Beau sat dejected, whining in the back seat.

"Oh, for pity's sake, moron. You'll see them again next week," Bertha said, watching him in the rearview mirror.

Beau didn't know how long that went on, going to the strange house to see Jo and Jack. Every time he had to leave them, he died a little more inside.

Why wouldn't anyone listen to him? He said he was sorry. He said he wouldn't do it again. Why wouldn't they let him go home? Why were they torturing him like that?

Jo and Jack asked the same questions.

Why wouldn't anyone listen to them? They said they were sorry. They'd be more careful in the future. Why wouldn't they let Beau come home? Why were they being so cruel?

Ms. Walters smiled in disgust at the sight of the trio. She shook her head. They didn't know how the game was played. Soon Beau would be placed in a home and the Canine Protection Services would get handsomely rewarded by the state for finding Beau a "safe" environment.

Silly, silly Jo and Jack. Silly Beau. It was better this way, they'd see. Ms. Walters knew best. After all, at twenty-four years of age, she knew a lot about being a proper caregiver. She had a puppy of her own, you see, and she knew. She knew.

Accidents didn't just happen. Someone was always to blame.

Beau no longer jumped and played. Bertha knew if Beau could be labeled as "special needs" she'd get a healthy bonus, so she took Beau to the vet without Jo and Jack's knowledge. She had Beau put on antidepressants. She got her hefty bonus every month. And Beau became apathetic.

One day, Bertha left the door open while she was out.

Beau poked his head out and sniffed around.

He didn't smell her.

"Dude. You don't want to be doing that," the gruff and tumbly bully-dog said.

Beau stuck his nose in the air and said, "Watch me," and bolted out the door.

Before long Ms. Walters showed up on Jo and Jack's doorstep, demanding Beau.

"Beau's not here," they told her truthfully.

Jo and Jack sat nervously waiting for Beau to come home. They put a bowl of water on the porch at night...just in case.

Ms. Walters called them the next day. "You'll be glad to know you're off the hook for dog-napping. Beau was found and was returned safely to Bertha's home."

"Why is he going back to Bertha's home? When he got out of our gate, you took him from us. Why aren't you taking him from Bertha? That doesn't make any sense."

"Oh, puppies get hurt or run away from foster care every day. Accidents happen. No one is to blame. We can't pull a puppy out of a foster home for that."

"Why not?" Jo grumbled. "You pulled him out of ours."

Days turned into weeks and weeks turned into months. Beau's coat was matted and dirty. His belly always felt as empty as his heart, and no one petted and loved on him. Bertha thought he had mental problems. She took him to the vet again.

Beau got more drugs from the vet. Bertha got more money from the state.

Beau sat in the corner most of the time, drugged out and angry. He no longer looked forward to visits with Jo and Jack because he knew they wouldn't last.

Just when he had given up all hope, Bertha loaded him up in the car and took him back to the fenced-in building.

She walked up the steps and dropped Beau in Jo's arms, turned around, and walked out.

Jo and Jack walked Beau back to their home. They bathed him and fed him and loved on him. They couldn't understand why he wouldn't play. They couldn't understand why he wasn't as happy as they were.

"You're home for good, Beau," they told him. "We won the court case. You don't need to worry anymore."

He didn't believe them. He couldn't believe them. He worried. He snarled and snapped at them. He no longer wagged his little tail.

Then the time came when Beau had to go outside to go potty.

He was terrified. What if they came back and took him? What if it was another trick?

He refused to step outside.

Beau piddled on the floor.

Ms. Walters walked in the door at that moment, as if she waited to pounce. She noticed the puddle on the floor and handed the girls another paper.

"See you in court," she said, as she snatched up Beau and marched out the door.

* * *

What? If you were expecting a happy ending, you're delusional. Everyone knows there are no happy endings when CPS gets involved.

California Burning

Top news story last week.

There was an earthquake (seven point something) in Indonesia last week, too, I think. I'm not really sure, because I saw it only once on the ticker tape. I guess no one got hurt or no one lost a home or maybe no Americans were put out by it.

We get a lot of fires in the Rockies. Earthquakes, too. Scary stuff—forces of nature.

The news coverage of the fire, albeit a bit overdone, was staggering. The pictures were awesome, (not in the sense of my children's definition (cool), but the true definition: inspiring an emotion of mingled reverence, dread, and wonder; fearful veneration or respect.)

Mother Nature has some pretty fierce and awesome elements: earth, wind, water, and fire.

California experienced more than its share of these elements what with all the quakes, landslides, mudslides, flooding, and now fire combined with gale-force winds. Not enough water and we die, too much water bids the same results.

It's that way with all of Mother Nature's gifts.

Moderation in all things is the key, so I've been told.

I lived in Southern California for about six years. Beautiful part of our country, isn't it? Peaches was born there. We lived through quite a few earthquakes and flash floods. I woke up riding my vibrating bed across my bedroom floor more than once. We never had to evacuate, though. Bonus!

On the news last week, I saw one family who put all of their precious belongings in their two cars and drove away to safety, only to be overcome by fire on their exit. They abandoned their cars and their belongings to the fire. Ironically, their home survived.

It started me thinking. (Oh, no. Here we go again.)

What would you take with you if you had to evacuate, not knowing if your house would survive?

My sister says she'd throw all the photo albums at her children and make sure they all got out with pictures in tow. I don't look good in pictures, so I don't think I'd mind much if all pictures of me burned. Doesn't almost everyone hate their own photograph...and recorded voice? Except children. They love to see their two-dimensional paper effigies and hear their voices emit from a box.

I believe pictures only capture the moment, not the essence of the moment. And certainly not the essence of your being.

My brother would probably ensure his puppy doggies and wife were safe before worrying about any of his belongings. (He has the cutest doggies... his wife's pretty cute, too.)

I don't have any doggies. I don't have a wife, either. We have two bunnies, though. The house would more than likely burn down while we tried to catch them. I'd probably open the gate and hope they survived.

My mom? Who knows? I guess my mom would like to take her books. She's been studying A Course in Miracles and a few other spiritually esoteric works of literature. I wouldn't know which couple of books to bring, I have so many. I'd probably be pondering the question as the house burnt down around me.

What would I pack?

I don't know.

If I didn't have a home, what good would stuff be? If the girls and I had no place to go, where would we place our knick-knacks?

Everything I have can be replaced. Even I can be replaced, according to my ex.

My stories are saved to the invisible and seemingly invincible filing cabinet of the Internet.

My family and friends are irreplaceable, but they aren't belongings, are they?

If I tried to pack up my children's precious belongings, I'd have to get a moving van. My girls think everything they own is precious and irreplaceable. They may be right.

I think I'd load up my car with food, water, dark chocolate...and toilet paper. [Sis thinks I have a preoccupation with potty humor.] Then, I'd sit in the car in the driveway, unsure of any destination, eating all the chocolate and wishing I'd bought more. Or maybe wishing I had marshmallows and graham crackers so the fire consuming my home would be maybe a little useful.

And then I'd wish I'd taken more pictures of my belongings so I could prove to the insurance company I really had all that crap I want them to replace – but they won't, because they're in the business of making money not replacing belongings. And even though I may have purchased that television for five hundred dollars two years ago, it's only worth fifty dollars now. And who cares if fifty dollars is nowhere close to replacing it, since I no longer own an entertainment center to house it in or a house to house the entertainment center in...

Besides, I left all of my pictures inside, didn't I?

...and I Know How to Use a Saw.

In my world, a self-sufficient, smart woman who takes personal responsibility for her actions ought to be at the top of the "desirable" list. Society ought to celebrate these women, regardless of their waist size or bra size... or how hot others deem them to be.

I have a dream that my five little girls will one day live in a nation where they will not be judged by the color of their hair or the size of their boobs, but by the content of their character.

What is this about, you ask? Get to the point, you say?

I am surrounded by what one may consider attractive women (and some not so attractive... some downright frumpy-dumpy), who are otherwise charming and engaging and pretty... until they open their mouths to speak, that is.

You know, I can plaster my walls, change my oil, change a flat, grow a garden, nurse a baby back to health, clean my house and all things in it. I can install a ceiling fan, unclog a drain, sew clothing, bake cakes, take out set-in stains... like blood... not that I've ever needed to... that you know... I can rake, mow, clip, trim, tile, glue, hammer, nail, sand paint... and I know how to properly use a saw.

I also know if you're gonna use "seen" in your sentence instead of saw, you always—without exception—have to use an auxiliary verb with it.

Everybody knows this, right? I mean, we learned this in fourth or fifth grade, right? After all, it's not rocket surgery.

American English. The language of the free, home of the brave.

I know you were teached correctly. I seen you sitting right there beside me in class; I seen the teacher write it on the board more then once... right before we done gone outside fer recess... Ain't I beautimous? I seen you lookin' at me. *wink, wink*

Who needs to use brains when you gots the parts with which all the boys want to tinker?

Yeah, I know how to use a saw... for all the good it does me.

Learning to Fly

Have you ever found yourself standing in a room full of passions you wanted to pursue and not knowing how to take that first step?

I've always wanted to learn to fly.

So, say you're standing in the middle of an Air & Space Museum, and you see that one sleek model. Stay clear it, girls. It has some tricky maneuvers. Tempting, yes, because it's beautiful. But, it's not your style. You don't even come close to its standards. And you doubt if you'd be able to handle it for long.

Then you spot an older model. But unfortunately, it has more in common with your mom... just sayin'. It's raring to go, but you have your reservations. It may get you up in the air, but it only has a couple flights left in it. You'll be tinkering with its engine more than you'll be enjoying air time. I know that's harsh, but... It is what it is.

And, then, much like Goldilocks, you find the perfect model. *The One*, and it's just right. It's your style. It's your speed. There's a mutual attraction. You could fly off into the sunset with this model.

Its engines are revved. You're standing so close you can touch it; you want so much to reach out to it—to feel it. Your heart is beating fast—too fast. This could be it. This could be the one to take you to new heights of passion. And, you've never wanted anything so much in your life.

Then you step back and look at all the other models in the room. And you see they all have pilots, and you realize even this one has a pilot. Not only do you not know how to fly, it isn't even yours to pilot if you did.

Its pilot has lovingly cared and tended this plane for years, which, if you were to be honest with yourself, is probably one of the reasons it's so appealing to you.

And then you see yourself clearly. You were never meant to fly, at least not a vessel as beautiful as this. You're not even qualified to sit in its cockpit. If you try to take this plane up in the air, you'll crash and burn—you don't know thing one about flying—ruining that fine craft in the process, destroying the dreams of its true pilot.

And, then you realize the price of your fancy is too steep for everyone.

It's a beautiful and worthy machine, but you're not.

And, you walk away.

Because you need to learn to fly before you start looking at planes.

Growing...Vertebrally Speaking

It all started about a week ago. I received a bizarre call from a psychotic dragon lady whose unfounded accusations need not be repeated. Suffice it to say, the conversation caught me totally off-guard. After that call, it seemed as if almost everything in my life went downhill.

A few weeks before, I had taken my car back to Ninth Street Radiator Repair to have the air conditioner compressor replaced. The air conditioner stopped working the previous summer. No one could find anything wrong with it at the time. Finally, the mechanic said it needed to be replaced at a cost of $650. I didn't have the funds, so I went without air conditioning until this year when I sold my youngest child and came up with the funds for the repair. The cost had somehow increased in a year to $850. But we don't have inflation, right?

It worked for a little over a week, thankfully, long enough to drive up to Wyoming and back.

Then it stopped working.

Just stopped. The day after the dragon lady called me. Me thinks her evil witch powers are great. The dark side of the force is strong with that one.

When my air conditioner stopped working, I called the dude at Ninth Street. I took it back. Seems it's a hose (the high-pressure hose) which is leaking, and they didn't know it had a leak until the pressure reached... blah, blah, blah.

I asked, "So could it have been the hose all along, and

not the compressor?"

Didn't really get an answer on that one.

He did state someone must have leaned on the hose and split it.

"Cool," said I. "Considering you and your boy have been the only people under my hood in over a year, do you think maybe one of you may have split it?"

"Just let me know when you'd like to get it fixed, or what you want to do about it."

Oh! And a big fat BTW! The hose itself costs over a hundred dollars.

Let's see: $350 last year for a "let's try it fix" which didn't. $850 for a new compressor which worked as well and as long as the "let's try it fix," and all the time and energy and doing without wheels. Shall I run back up to Ninth Street Radiator and plunk down at least another Benjamin?

What's a girl to do? I'll let you know when I figure it out. As for now, I really am one hot momma!

I have a catalpa tree growing in my backyard. It's a little sprout nicely snuggled in the corner of my property. I like it. It'll give wonderful shade in a couple of years. My goal is to make a backyard retreat, hidden from snooping eyes.

Speaking of snooping eyes, my next-door neighbor Beulah, who is eighty-six now, told me she didn't want me growing a catalpa tree. She sees them as messy and doesn't want it to litter her yard. She asked if she could cut it. I told her I'd like to let it grow out a bit, and then I would have it trimmed up in about a year, once I knew it would survive.

By the way, I know all about neighbor's trees littering one's yard. Beulah has two humongous sick elms which litter my yard with sticky dead leaves all spring, summer, and autumn. Whenever I step outside barefoot to change the water hose position, I have to peel layers of blechhhy leaves off my feet. It's the price of living in a neighborhood. You deal.

With all the minutia going on in my life, it felt as if my life was a stacking up like a pile of cold pancakes just dripping with despair.

I stepped outside yesterday on my way to work and noticed my baby catalpa was sheared on the neighbor's side, and over twelve inches into my yard.

One might say it's such a stupid thing to get upset about, but it made me cry. I can't explain it. I started bawling. Like a frickin' baby. And I couldn't stop.

I wrote a note to un-home my neighbor (and it's verbatim. I saved it. I can prove it):

"Hey Beulah, I hope you're doing well. I asked you to please not cut my tree because it's still so little. Please don't. I don't want it to die. Thank you. I appreciate it. Sandi"

When I came home from work yesterday, Beulah was still un-home, but I had an answer written on the back of my note, taped to my back door, written by her daughter.

"Sandy"... yeah, she didn't notice I spell my name with an "i" because like most self-ass-orbed people, they don't give a damn about anyone but themselves, their things, and their wants. [Disclaimer: I don't really care how you spell my name, but if you get a note from Ethel, you don't want to reply to Ethyl, I'm just saying.]

"Sandy, I spent almost two hours last week trimming the bushes that had grown over from your side of the fence onto Mom's side, preventing her from easily getting to her trash can and alley access. Our trash man hauled away three cans full of the trimmings. Please keep the branches trimmed from now on. Mom has told you that she doesn't want the catalpa branches to come over onto her property because catalpas are a messy tree. Please keep the branches trained to your side. (By the way, I have seen a calalpa [sic] resurrect itself from a stump. They're impossible to kill.). Cathy"

I called the city and asked about the municipal code on such matters. An officer of the law came out to inspect the damage. I learned quite a few things from Officer JC yesterday afternoon.

Did you know it's not your responsibility to keep your bushes off your neighbor's lawn? That's on them. If they don't want foliage to intrude on their space which may prevent one from trash cans and alley access, they alone are responsible for clipping them, or moving their trash can to a more accessible area, whichever is easier. Oh, by the way, the bushes she's complaining about (not that it matters much) are out of control sprouts from Beulah's own elm trees. I've tried everything to kill the buggers, to no avail.

If your foliage is intruding on their space, they are allowed to cut it, even if you don't want it cut. But—and she has a big butt—they are not allowed to venture even a millimeter over onto your side of the property. By coming in a foot from the fence line onto my legal property to trim my baby catalpa, Wonder Woman plopped herself down in the "wrong!" category.

The irony here is I've done so much for Beulah when she needed it over the years. If she needed something done in the past, she would call me when her daughter was unavailable (read, frequently). I'm heartbroken. Cathy had to trim the bushes for her eighty-six-year-old mother. Oh, the humanity!

Officer JC gave me a little courage. I wrote another note because Beulah is still un-home. I'm thinking she's on vaca and her loverly daughter is taking care of the place while she's away.

"Cathy..." I maybe ought to have written "Cathi"... hrm... too late now. Anyway...

"Cathy, according to municipal code, any branches which hang over to your (Beulah's) side of the property are your responsibility, not mine. As for my tree, you are not legally within your rights to reach over to trim my tree. You may only cut branches and leaves which hang over your property. Please refrain from clipping my tree in the future. If you feel a leaf or random branch which hangs over your property causes you strife, feel free to cut it as long as you not venture over my legal property line. By the way, I don't want a stump in my yard. I want a (not-deformed) catalpa tree. Sand i"

Some of you may incorrectly state it's Karma coming back at me full force. I disagree wholeheartedly.

I think the Universe offers situations which, by how we act, can either teach us to be stronger or allows us to whimper away, defeated and a lesser person.

Dragon Lady started it by shrieking sick accusations via Ma Bell. I did what I always do when anyone yells at me over the phone: I hung up, and whimpered away a defeated and lesser person. I ought to have stood up for myself and told her what a sick, deranged individual she was for even considering such. The lesson may have stopped there.

But I didn't. I reacted ...well, I'm not proud of the way I handled that situation, therefore the Universe stuck another test in my path, my car's broken air conditioner. I still haven't faced that challenge. So once more my personal rights have been violated in the shape of a vulnerable baby catalpa tree.

I think I'm finally learning the lesson. I feel my spine strengthening a little bit every day. We shall see.

Who says you can't teach an old dog new tricks?

All You Can Be

An acquaintance approached me the other day who doesn't really much care for my outspoken, abrupt personality. (By the way, "doesn't much care for" is me being polite. I truly believe she despises me.) She was kindly generous with her compliments regarding my nomination for my last book award. She spoke to me a little about her dream of writing her own book(s), but for some reason hadn't quite finished.

The world is full of people with dreams such as these, I believe.

To be quite frank with you, I, too, am hugely insecure about my talents. These doors which are currently opening up to me are smacking me in the face. I question my talent. And during those frail times I hear my father's voice inside my head. "Who the hell do you think you are? You aren't any good. What makes you think anyone would want to read anything you write? Why, if I wanted to write a book it'd be ten times better than anything you could scribble."

And it promptly pushes my proud self back on my ass.

Then I hear another's voice. "It's just your little hobby. When're you going to get a real job? If it weren't for me, you wouldn't have been able to write any books. Hell, I practically wrote those books for you. I should win the awards."

I guess my point is, you can't let these people trample your drive. You're probably too hard on yourself already.

Think to yourself, "If I don't try, where might I be in a year?" The answer is probably right about where you are now.

Then ask yourself, "If I do try, where might it take me?" Oh, the possibilities.

The other day President Obama told our children to forgo any hopes of being the next JLo (I'm paraphrasing a bit—please forgive) and to study, because studying and achieving will get you a useful degree which will lead to a productive life for this country of ours. I'm not saying he's wrong, but let me put it this way:

Jo came home from school after they aired his speech and she asked, "Why would he tell us to not pursue our dreams? What right does he have to say I'm probably not going to make it as a singer?"

You know, I listened to his speech. I heard him say it's better to stay in school than to drop out to pursue any kind of pipe-dream, because chances are you're not going to be the next *American Idol*... but it didn't register in my mind as anything wrong or disingenuous.

Then I heard his message from Jo's perspective, and she's right. What right does anyone (President or father or others) have to tell anyone to forget following their dreams because they'll never be as good as the best.

So what?

The "best" is subjective and is never static. I suppose you could be the best poop sculptor, as no one really wants to sculpt poop, until someone sees you sculpting poop (or plucks that random poop-sculpting thought from the Universal Stream of Consciousness) and sculpts a better poop statue than you. (You know, if you say "sculpt" enough times it sounds like a made-up word?)

What I'm trying to say is: it doesn't matter.

Write that book.

Play that guitar.

Paint that picture.

Sing your little heart out, if that's what makes you real,

if that's what gives you reason to breathe.

Stop listening to those well-meanies who say stuff like, "I don't know who said you could sing, but they lied to you."

Take a page from that shoe company and just do it.

What have you done to achieve your goals today?

(Yeah, me neither. Got to get right on that.)

Cup of Kindness

I read an obituary from a neighboring town for a lady who lived to be ninety-three. She lived and worked all her life in the town in which she was born. From all appearances she looked as if she'd not really accomplished much. She worked her entire adult life as a waitress in various venues. The article didn't mention any formal higher education.

The posted picture showed a kind and gentle face smiling at the camera, gently lined with wrinkles.

The article said she was loved by many and would be missed by everyone in the town; they all knew her by name and remembered her fondly.

You think about a remarkable life. You ponder about what makes fame or how to measure success.

I wonder if she considered herself successful.

She'll be missed by thousands who knew her by name... thousands. Yet, she didn't build any cathedrals or fly a plane across the Atlantic. She didn't write a best-seller, or sing like an angel on stage. You'll not find her on the silver screen or standing behind a politician's podium. She wasn't a prestigious CEO. She didn't make a six-figure income or live in a mansion.

But I bet she kept your coffee cup topped off and knew exactly what you wanted for breakfast by the look on your face or the temperature outside. She could serve you up a smile on the gloomiest of days and never utter a harsh word to even the most cantankerous customer. And I imagine she never felt as if she was a less-than or treated anyone else like one, either.

You could measure success by the number of bodies you trample to get to the top. You might consider yourself successful by rubbing elbows with the creamiest of the crop and turning your nose up at your employees or the hotel maids or the rest of the ribble-rabble you consider to be less-thans. You can put all the pretty little initials you want behind your name, but I can guarantee the people attending her funeral will be there because they loved and respected her in life. The people at your funeral will be there because they're expected to be.

So how do you measure success? Is it in the kind memories and warm thoughts you leave behind in others, those whose hearts fill with love at the thought of you? Or is it measured by the title you procure in your career, the highest rung you achieve on the corporate ladder, the number of lowly less-than employees you can bully and ignore on your trek to greatness?

I have no answer. The careerly (it's a word now) successful have buildings named after them. Sometimes they secure that honor in life by having a building remodeled while they hold the highest office, allowing them to receive the credit and accolades, complete with their pretty, little names on a big shiny plaque for all to admire. Other times they donate obscene amounts of money to have something built in their honor. In essence, their names live on for centuries, barring the zombie apocalypse.

I have no illusions about my own impact on this world. If I have a funeral, it more than likely won't be attended by many. There should be coffee, though. It wouldn't be right not to have coffee…and maybe some good coffee crumb cake. Hot and cinnamon-y. That would be nice. Wine, maybe, too.

Anyway, I'm envious of this woman who, in the typically successful person's eyes, didn't amount to much during her ninety-three years on this planet.

She's contributed more to this world than the best of the elite. And although I never met her, she's earned my respect. It's more than I can say for any executive, at least any I've worked for.

She should at least have a tasty sandwich named after her, that's all I'm saying.

Sandwiches are more functional than plaques.

One of Your Five

I know I'm one of your five.

I figured it out about ten years ago when you got a computer and social media savvy.

You send me a post weekly (at least) telling me if I don't send it on to five (more is better) of my favorite people, all hell will break loose. But it's okay because God ...or Nieman Marcus sent it to you apparently, and you want to ensure I'll receive the money, hopes, answered prayers and cookie recipes promised in said email by sending it on.

Well, I'm here to tell you I fell for that the first couple of years. And like a moron, I posted it on to my fave five, plus back to you as instructed. And much like the *Publishers Clearing House Sweepstakes* claim I won five bazillion bucks, nothing happened.

At least I don't think so.

Maybe I've been staying alive only because of those posts. Or maybe I'm still alive as punishment for not sending them on. Maybe I was supposed to meet my maker and exist in blissful immortality picking silver fruits from golden trees in the kingdom of heaven.

Anyway. Thank you.

Your emails saved my life...or kept me from dying. Either way, I am none the wiser.

Send them to me if you must. I'll ignore them and steady myself for the eventual apocalypse from my inaction.

(I live on the edge.)

What's So Funny?

I'm sitting here not knowing what to do with myself because Jack isn't reading over my shoulder and interjecting with her usual, "Momma, I'm hungry." Or "Momma, when's lunch?"

My eldest is pregnant with my second grandson. She told me they've (tentatively) decided to name the baby Noah.

"Great," I said. "Now I'll have to buy him two of everything."

My mom has a friend, Lorena, who is in her late eighties. Apparently, Lorena's not doing too well. The other day Mom told me Lorena is now on oxygen.

I replied, "Aren't we all?"

I went to the local Office Depot to replace my phone adapter the other day. I asked the salesmanpersonthingy if they had any USB cables. He said, "Sure do. How long do you need it?"

And swear to God I said, "Oh, about four years ought to do it."

He shook his head and said, "You're killing me, here."

I know it's an old joke, but it had to be said. He just handed the line to me—without a care in the world as to how I'd use it. The groan belongs to him.

But the biggest joke of all continues to be the pharma-ceutical companies which place ads for their snake oils on the television and in our magazines, knowing full-well we cannot buy said poisons without a note from our doctors.

I guess the joke's on us, really, because we lemmings see and hear the ads, ignoring the pill's death wishes disguised as "side-effect may include," and we arrive at our doctors' offices armed with false expectations of drugs our bodies have no use for.

It seems like pharmaceutical companies and doctors these days don't really give a shit about us or our health.

Just the health of our bank accounts...

Next.

Frustration

I wrap my fingers around you.

I've longed for the feel of you in my
hands; your hardness pleases me.

I caress you while I imagine the heights you'll take me.

I slide you in...

I slide you out, ever... so... slowly...

I position you. I pause...

My heart beats a bit faster. My breath catches.

I bite my lip.

I'm not quite ready. It's been a while...

Slower... we have time.

I slide you in, and hold you there.

The seconds pass.

I sense your energy;

Our potential

I dare not move

for fear of ruining this perfect moment.

I slide you out.

I bring you to my lips;my tongue plays with your
tip and my lips barely dance across your shaft. My
mind is already where we could be together.

Okay. I'm ready.

I place your tip in the proper position and slowly
move with you. With every stroke I become
more excited, more alive... more me.

My passion pours out through you.

Each stroke melds us, you and me. Entangled in
a divine purpose, fate brought us together.

I feel your power as you allow me to guide you.

My hunger builds.

Our strokes come faster now,

more powerful, raw with desire.

My mind races, my heart pounds,

I grip you tighter.

I am lost in the moment with you.

The phone screams from its cradle

...My passion evaporates; gone.

I slide you back into your cap,

and place you on our half-written page.

There will be no more writing today.

About the Author

Sandra Miller Linhart was born and raised in a somewhat isolated, but beautiful, mountainous town in Wyoming. There she cultivated her love of the written word, as the nearest decent record store was a good two-hour drive away and the one local radio station played only country and classical music at that time. Were it not for that, Ms. Linhart might today be a rock star, or, at the very least have better taste in music.

As it turned out, Lander provided a well-stocked and constantly updated library. Thus, the young Ms. Linhart often found herself taking long journeys into the wonderful worlds created by authors like Ursula K. LeGuin, Judy Blume, Madeleine L'Engle, Stephen King and, of course, Erma Bombeck in the dusty basement which contained the children's section of the Fremont County Public Library.

Sandra then traveled the country as a military wife and mother of five army brats; soaking in our country's diverse and obscure cultural differences—which makes wonderful fodder for her stories.

She currently lives in the mountains of Colorado but spends a majority of her time at the beach.

Sandra writes in hopes of sharing her love of reading and writing with everyone. She utilizes her sociology degree and personal experience in writing children's books for caregivers, parents, and children to better connect and communicate, with the goal of healing anxieties and fears. She loves to write for children of all ages, and plans to do so until her last page is turned.

Life (and how *you* live it) is her inspiration. Visit her website: www.sandstarbooks.com

www.ingramcontent.com/pod-product-compliance
Lightning Source LLC
Chambersburg PA
CBHW071346290326
41933CB00041B/2704